Martha Black

Martha Louise Black on her seventieth birthday.

Northern History Library

Martha
Black

MARTHA
LOUISE
BLACK

Edited and updated
by Flo Whyard

Alaska Northwest Publishing Company
Edmonds, Washington

My Seventy Years, by Mrs. George Black, F.R.G.S. (as told to
Elizabeth Bailey Price), was published in 1938 by Thomas Nelson and
Sons Ltd.

First Printing May 1976
Revised Edition 1986

Library of Congress Cataloging-in-Publication Data

Black, Martha Louise, 1866-1957.
    Martha Black.

    (Northern history library)
    Rev. ed. of: My ninety years. c1976.
    1. Frontier and pioneer life — Yukon Territory.
2. Klondike River Valley (Yukon) — Gold discoveries.
3. Yukon Territory — History.   4. Black, Martha
Louise, 1866-1957.   5. Yukon Territory — Biography.
I. Whyard, Florence. II. Black, Martha Louise,
1866-1957. My ninety years. III. Title. IV. Series.
F1091.B528   1986   971.9'102'0924 [B]   86-22328
ISBN 0-88240-062-2

Book Editor: By Fish
Cover design by Sandra Harner
Book design by David A. Shott
Alaska Northwest Publishing Company
130 Second Avenue South
Edmonds, Washington 98020

Printed in U.S.A.

CONTENTS

First Lady of The Yukon . . . Martha Louise Black, wife of the Commissioner of Yukon, in a beaded tea gown, ready to receive guests at Government House.

FOREWORD

Martha Louise Black, an American of pre-Revolution ancestry, a background of finishing school and other proper social connections through family and friends, was a most unlikely person to trudge over Chilkoot Pass at the height of the gold rush to the Yukon in 1898. It was equally remarkable that at the age of 70 she should be elected Yukon's Member of the Canadian Parliament, to serve for five years.

That was when Flo Whyard, journalist in naval uniform during World War II and a member of the Canadian Women's Press Club in Ottawa, met Mrs. Black, who put on an annual dinner for the press women. "She cast a spell over me that grew stronger through the years," Flo says. "There was an instant affinity with anyone who interviewed her, and I felt it very strongly when I knew her in Whitehorse in later years."

In Whitehorse Flo interviewed Martha several times for the Canadian Broadcasting Company, one occasion being the celebration of her 90th birthday. Mrs. Black had counted on becoming that age and planned to reissue her book, *My Seventy Years*, under the title *My Ninety Years*. She did not manage it before her death at 91, in 1957.

From the interviews, and as "an avid fan" who had gathered many anecdotes about the Blacks, Flo was familiar with the events in Martha's final 20 years and the stories she had hoped to tell about that part of her life. At the time, though, no publisher was interested in reprinting an old book with the addition of new but unfinished chapters. If the project were ever to be completed, it was up to Flo Whyard.

When George Black died in 1962 and a sale of family possessions was held, she added to her already extensive collection of material by obtaining Mrs. Black's parliamentary diary for 1937, her set of *Encyclopedia Britannica* with its bookcase, and one of her flower books. For a Christmas gift, Flo's husband Jim tracked down a copy of Martha's *My Seventy Years,* written in collaboration with Elizabeth Bailey Price. It was long out of print and if a copy could be found these days, a collector might pay as much as $75 for it.

Flo continued to do research for an epilogue that would cover those last two decades and thus, in its own way, fulfill Mrs. Black's dream. She studied microfilm, dug up photographs and correspondence, gathered newspaper clippings and interviewed those who had known the Blacks. As she said throughout, it was all "a labour of love." If she found a publisher, the royalties would go to one of Mrs. Black's favorite organizations, the Imperial Order Daughters of the Empire.

During this period Flo became Canadian editor for *ALASKA* ® magazine, published by Alaska Northwest Publishing Company. When ANWP entered the book field in earnest, with a growing list of titles, it was decided that since Martha Louise Black was an amazing woman in Yukon history her autobiography should not remain out of print. In this reissue it has been condensed to eliminate references to passing events too far in the past to be familiar to readers today. Otherwise the text follows the original, to portray the attitudes and writing style of the period as well as its actual events. To better tell Mrs. Black's story, additional photos have been included in this reissue.

Even as final preparations for publication were under way, another sequel developed, one that should prove Mrs. Black did, indeed, influence her young friend. Let Flo Whyard tell it:

"Because Martha blazed her political trail at the age of 70, I felt I could run as a candidate for Yukon Council at the age of 58. [She was elected and now serves in the Territory's legislature.]

"Each time I read her book, I find another special little bit of closeness between us. So will every woman who has the opportunity to read *Martha Black*. She has so much to say to us."

By Fish, *Book Editor, 1976*
Alaska Northwest Publishing Company

ACKNOWLEDGMENTS

Many friends have made this new edition possible: Mary Mac-Bride Botthof of Reno, Nevada, who produced the original photos, typescript and other memorabilia from her mother's papers; Iris Warner and staff members at the Yukon Archives, whose long hours of rewarding search produced many relevant historic photos; former Yukon Commissioner and Mrs. Fred Collins, who loaned personal souvenirs of their warm friendship with the Blacks; G.I. and Martha Cameron, who helped in identification of photos and filled in many missing gaps; my husband, who painstakingly copied old photos and provided continued support in the project over many years; and finally, Robert A. Henning, whose generosity made this new edition a possibility.

My only regret is that it will not be possible to hand Martha Black the first copy off the press and watch the twinkle in her eye when she says, "Well, it's about time!"

Flo Whyard
Whitehorse, Yukon

Young sister Belle Torrence Munger, with Martha Louise. There was 17 years between them and Martha had never lived at home while Belle was growing up. As Martha wrote, she never really had a sister in her early years, little lame Agnes having died in infancy.

Chapter I
I AM BORN

The first story told about me concerns my birth. This was related by Aunt Agnes, Father's eldest sister, who, standing by the bedside of a frightened 16-year-old mother, said, "Susan, shall I call George?"

"Yes," whispered the tearful, exhausted girl-wife; "but I am so sorry. He won't be pleased."

Father came into the room and kissed Mother gravely. He looked at his twin girl babies and said, "Susan, I am disappointed. I expected a boy."

"Yes, I know, I am so sorry."

"If my husband had said that to me I would have thrown those two babies at him," I afterwards told Mother. Her eyes filled with tears as she quietly remarked, "Not at a man like your dear father."

I am sure that Father did not mean to be hard or cruel, but he had the fixed idea of the men of that day, that woman was created for the sole purpose of ministering to the physical comfort and desires of man. He admired intelligent women, but at the same time they annoyed him. He expected women to be good housekeepers, wives, and mothers.

I am a member of the ninth American-born generation of Mungers. According to the *Book of Munger*, which is a record of my paternal family tree and traditions, Nicholas Munger, the progenitor of the name in United States, came to America in 1645, at the age of 16 years. He was one of the first settlers of the Guildford Colony, in what today is the state of Connecticut.

My forebears fought in the American Revolution, the War of 1812, and the Civil War. Among them were pioneers, patriots, slave-owners and abolitionists, farmers, industrialists, preachers, teachers, poets, sailors, and soldiers. Father's great-grandmother, Abigail Button, was a connection of Button Gwynette, one of the signers of the Declaration of Independence.

I have always been proud of my people and their service to their country. I feel honoured indeed that I inherit from them the distinction of the right to be a governor's daughter, a Colonial Dame, and a Daughter of the American Revolution.

Mother was the daughter of John W. Owens, owner of a large plantation and several Ohio River packets—a member of the family which founded Owensville, Kentucky, where she was born. Her mother was Mary Ludlow Cummins of Ohio, after whom Cumminsville was named. Her grandmothers, Jeanette Cummins and Susan Ludlow, were accredited to be the mothers of the first white boy and first white girl born in Cincinnati. For years portraits of these grandmothers, bequeathed by Grandfather Owens to the Young Men's Mercantile Library Association, hung in the Cincinnati City Hall.

On the death of her father in 1864, to settle his estate, Mother and her two sisters were brought back to Owensville by Uncle and Aunt Mary Ann Howells (parents of William Dean). It was during the Civil War, which had considerably depreciated her father's property, and the three orphans went at once to live with Aunt Fanny Fosdick (wife of Admiral Fosdick) and Uncle Henry Pearce in Cincinnati.

At the time Father, who had been wounded at the battle of Seven Pines, was convalescing in this border city, where Northerners and Southerners mingled.

Father met Mother, and they fell in love. Shortly afterwards, in the face of bitter opposition, they were married—Mother, a Southerner, barely 16, Father, a Northerner, 12 years her senior. It was a "Yankee" marriage which aroused all Mother's kin to fury. Father could provide neither a home nor the comforts to which she had been accustomed.

But Mother shared the vicissitudes of his life lovingly and trustfully. She uttered no complaint about going to Chicago, and here in February 1866 my twin sister and I, Martha Louise Munger, were born.

I never knew my twin sister as she lived only a few hours. Many times I have longed for her, have imagined the good times we might have had together, the companionship, the unity of understanding, the love that is the heritage of twins.

Mother was slow in regaining her strength. Now I can see that her youth, her early training, her sheltered life, were poor preparation to meet the hardships of the Midwest as the wife of a poor man.

Other children came so quickly in those first four years. All these, save myself and my little lame sister Agnes, who lived to be three, died in infancy. I have often heard mother say, "In four years I had five children."

Such records as the survival of one baby of five, all born within four years are common records of past generations.

Father and Mother had many definite theories of child-training, and I, their eldest, bore the brunt of these. One of Father's pet sayings was, "Someday one of my girls may be the wife of the President of United States and live in the White House, and I want her to know how to fill a position like that. On the other hand, one of my girls may have to work for the President's wife, and I want her to know how to do that equally well."

Now I realize that I had a wonderful father and mother. I know that they did all they could to make my childhood happy and to fit me in every way to meet life. My greatest wish for the children of today is that their training may be as balanced a combination of discipline and pleasure as mine was.

My first vivid childhood memory is a mad race before the fierce flames of the great Chicago fire; of our family fleeing for safety to the sandy shores of Lake Michigan. I can scarcely breathe. I am coughing, sputtering, and my eyes are stinging almost unbearably from the smoke. (I was five years old, and it was the morning of the second day of the fire, Monday, October 9, 1871.)

I remember that the night before I was awakened by an unusual commotion in the house. Our Irish cook, Hannah, had come home from church crying. A fire had started in a barn near by, had spread quickly to her church, and burned it to the ground. I recall sitting on Mother's knee, in a rocking-chair, in the big bay window of our West Van Buren Street home, watching the sky grow redder and redder, and seeing high tongues of flame shooting through great black smoky clouds, and huge burning brands carried through the air by the terrific wind that shook the house.

Through a haze of 65 years it is hard to separate my actual memories of one of the greatest fires in history from the many stories told in my home so often. But I do remember some of the horrible sights of that ghastly flight. People with black and blood-stained faces, dragging or carrying frightened, screaming children

3

. . . sick people carried on stretchers . . . others pulling baby carriages, wheelbarrows or hand wagons, loaded with a few precious possessions . . . families like ours, who had the ready money to hire carts or wagons. All hurrying, hurrying, as though pursued by a demon. And what a terrible demon it was! We could feel its hot breath suffocating us, stinging our eyes to tears which ran down our smoke-blackened faces.

I still recall the awful noises: the roar of the fire . . . the frightened crying and hysterical sobbing of children . . . the screaming of stampeding horses . . . the bellowing of cattle, broken loose from the stockyards.

At last we reach the lake shore . . . as far away from the fire as possible. . . .

We lived three days in the open on the lake shore. Our men kept our fire going night and day with wood from wood piles which grew bigger every day from the many logs and kindlings dumped upon them. I liked this life. I had always wanted to live outside. I liked getting all our food from the big wagons. I liked baking potatoes in an outside fire, and I always asked Hannah to let me tend them.

The nights grew colder and we lived in tents until our new house was finished. As fast as possible the city was building small houses for the homeless on Wapense Avenue (now 37th Street), and we were to have one of four rooms to ourselves, because there were seven of us. Father was angry that they were already calling the district "Poverty Flats." Our shanty there was indeed a contrast to our storey-and-a-half frame home on West Van Buren Street.

Looking up statistics, I note that 98,500 people were burned out, 21,800 downtown residents were rendered homeless, more than 250 counted dead, and approximately $200 million of property destroyed. The charity of the American people and of other countries was unprecedented. Food, clothing, and supplies of every kind valued at over $7 million poured into the stricken city.

The spirit of the Chicago people was undaunted, and rebuilding began at once. Within a year a far greater city, with fireproof buildings, sprang phoenix-like from the ruins.

Today some of my most cherished possessions are grandmother's spoons, and some fine pieces of linen, now yellow with age, which had been hastily thrown into the wagon on the occasion of that mad race for life before the Chicago fire.

I have always felt that I am fortunate in belonging to a family which had so much of the Scottish clan spirit—a connection is a connection, whether rich or poor, in success or in adversity. I am sure that Father's and Mother's relatives were pillars of strength to them in those dire days of Poverty Flats, especially the Morses, who lived in Chicago.

Uncle Charles Hosmer Morse, son of a Vermont clergyman, was certainly one of America's self-made men. I have heard him tell of the time he began to work for the Fairbanks Company as an office sweeper in their New York office. He was wearing a homespun suit, and his fellow-workers made fun of his clothes. But when he died the "country bumpkin" was president and 90 per cent owner of the Fairbanks-Morse Company.

We did not live long in Poverty Flats. Grandfather Munger and Uncle Charles Morse came to Father's rescue financially, and he re-established his laundry business. He had an exceptionally good business head, and the setback of the fire aroused his fighting spirit and challenged him to greater efforts. Business boomed again, and we moved to "our nice new house" on North Franklin Street, near Lincoln Park—a brick English basement house, with brownstone trimmings and a cupola.

Opposite us lived Levi Z. Leiter, one of the founders of Marshall Field, which was originally Field and Leiter. Across a hollow lot were the Vaughans and the Buschs, one of the Anheuser Busch firm. Father and the heads of these three families united in having their various hired men flood the hollow lot to make a skating rink for us children.

I used to admire the elegant Miss Mary Victoria Leiter, who later, as the wife of Lord Curzon, Viceroy of India, became an important social leader.

My grandparents, Mr. and Mrs. Lyman Munger, played an important part in my early training. They had moved from New England in the early years of their married life to the oilfields at Mercer, Pennsylvania. After the fire there the year I was born, they took up residence in Galva, Illinois, where grandfather practised his profession of apothecary in his own drug store.

They visited us often in Chicago. They took me to my first circus when I was eight years old. I recall that it was the captive balloon that fascinated me more than anything else. You could go up for a quarter and get a flag besides. The conversation went like this:

Mattie: "Oh, grandfather, please let me go up."

Grandmother: "Certainly not! Come, Mattie, you can have a ride on the merry-go-round."

We all went away.

I could not get the balloon out of my mind . . . grandfather and grandmother were looking away . . . I had my own quarter . . . I hurried back to the balloon . . . I got there just as it was ready to go up . . . I bought my ticket and got my flag. The balloon ascended, and I was thrilled to my innermost being. I looked down and saw my grandparents looking for me. I shouted and waved my flag at them. The balloon descended, and I was met with an ominous silence. I was taken home immediately. Grandfather escorted me to the little arbour (the scene of all corporal punishment) where I received one of his mild spankings—the kind that never really hurt.

Even now I boast that never could a person get more for a quarter: a balloon ride, a flag, and spanking. "That's your money's worth," say I.

When my brother George Merrick was born, because of Mother's long illness I went to live with my grandparents in Galva. Every afternoon grandfather read two hours, his favourite authors being Scott, Thackeray, and Dickens. I used to sit on a small stool sewing my "stint," a perforated cardboard motto with wool cross stitch. Many a "God Bless Our Home" and "Welcome to Our Home" I've made.

An instance of grandfather's intuitive knowledge of child psychology comes to me. My Uncle Charles Morse had given me my first diamonds, at the age of 14 years—a pair of pin-point diamond earrings. My vanity rose to that; and I must have my ears pierced.

Mother was goaded to the point of making it an issue: that it was utterly preposterous for a girl of 14 to have her ears pierced and wear diamond earrings.

Grandfather, who was visiting us at the time, said, "Susan, I think you are a little hard on Mattie. I'd let her have her ears pierced. But, you know, it is a very delicate business, and sometimes ears get infected. You remember the case in the paper the other day of a girl who had to have a poisoned ear cut right off. I myself would like to pierce Mattie's ears, to avoid any possible danger of bloodpoisoning."

I beamed on grandfather.

"Now, Mattie, we'll do this on a Saturday, which will allow you Saturday and Sunday to get over your suffering, because it will hurt. But you won't mind that, because you want to wear your diamond earrings, don't you?"

I nodded.

Saturday comes. Grandfather prepares. When I arrive, I see a log, a three-cornered sail needle threaded with a piece of heavy waxed silk, a wooden mallet, and a piece of leather, over which grandfather has placed a small piece of linen. I look at this.

"Now, Mattie, come here. I will rub the lobe of your ear until it is numb. You will then place it upon the linen, and with one blow on the needle, and a quick jerk of it to pull the thread, the trick is done. Your ear will not hurt for a few seconds because it will be numb, but you will suffer, and you must be prepared to stand the pain and soreness for at least two days."

I think of the skating party that afternoon.

"Grandfather, couldn't we wait until next week?"

"Certainly," he replies.

And so it went on for days. "Mattie, have you time today to get your ears pierced?" was the daily question. In the meantime all the horrible details of painful piercings, even fatal results, were incidental bits of family conversation.

Time went on and on. Then one day grandfather said, "Now Mattie, since you never seem to have time to get your ears pierced, wouldn't it be nice to get your earrings made into a pretty brooch?" I acceded joyfully. To this day it is one of my treasures. And I haven't had my ears pierced yet!

After two years in high school I was placed in the Lake Forest Select Seminary for Young Ladies, to be "finished." Looking backward, I think I nearly finished those in charge of the "Select Seminary." I was continually getting into escapades. I was not disobedient, but my troubles arose from my zest for adventure. When seized by the urge of a particular quest, in pursuit of it I forgot all rules and regulations, thereby upsetting the discipline of the school. My teachers complained so often that finally my parents became too distraught to defend me and I was taken out.

It was then that Mother thought of her convent education, under the supervision of the Sisters of the Holy Cross in France. She talked over this type of school with Father, who agreed that certainly some more effective discipline was sadly needed for me. There were schools, directed by this same order of Sisters in the United States, the Mother house being St. Mary's of Notre Dame,

7

Indiana, a school of high repute throughout the country. They decided to send me there.

I spent five of the grandest years of my life at St. Mary's. I was thrilled by the beauty of its setting—the loveliness and fragrance of the "mile of lilacs" driveway—the woodland paths, the winding St. Joseph's River, and the beautiful flower gardens.

Great stress was laid on our "deportment." We were trained for every kind of social function, especially a royal drawing-room, as most of the girls hoped to be presented at Court. I suppose I have made a thousand curtsies to the picture of Queen Victoria. With sheets pinned around our waists with safety-pins, to form court trains, dear little Sister Ignatia, our deportment teacher, taught us to make a low curtsy and retire several feet gracefully. I have been glad of this training since.

Of all studies, I enjoyed elocution most. I still have my old elocution book, one which had been Mother's. It is inscribed with her name, "Susan Owens," in fine delicate penmanship, followed by my small vertical, round, "positive" signature—our handwriting significant of Mother's reserve and my aggressiveness.

The second subject of interest was botany, and St. Mary's grounds were a floral paradise. As a child I had always loved flowers, and was forever picking them and hunting for four-leaf clovers. I remember once telling Father I could find a hundred. He, thinking to impress on me the folly of exaggerated statements, said, "Daughter, I do not agree, but I will give you a dollar for every four-leaf clover you find." Before the end of the second day I had gathered over 50. Father paid me the money and asked to be released from his bargain, declaring he had enough good luck to last all the rest of his life.

Father and Mother, both naturally hospitable, encouraged me to invite my schoolmates home for weekends and holidays. Indeed, ever since I can remember, if "sudden company" appeared at meal-time, Mother always invited them to share the meal. "Always ask a meal-time visitor to eat with you—even if you are only having baked potatoes," she impressed upon us. "Remember, what is good enough for the family is good enough for a guest—and never, never apologize for simple meals."

Father arranged many happy holiday times for me and my friends. He took us regularly to hear Stoddart's lectures. Once he had a party at our home in honour of Sir Henry Stanley, who visited

Chicago after one of his African trips. A prized possession today is an autographed copy of *In Darkest Africa*, bearing the inscription, "To the Young Daughter of my Friend George Munger."

During holidays I was allowed to go to a few evening student parties at the homes of relatives and family friends, but until I was 18 I had never been out later than midnight. Mother, being very delicate ever since my brother George was born, could not chaperone me, but Father always took me and called for me. When I was telling this to a young woman the other day she remarked, "And now we go for the fathers."

It was at one of these parties I met handsome Will Purdy, a student at the Morgan Park Military Academy, and son of Warren G. Purdy, president of the Chicago Rock Island and Pacific Railway, and prominent in military and masonic circles. We at once became friends.

My five years at St. Mary's flew by, and I graduated in June 1886, the proud possessor of an elocution medal with three bars, an essay medal with one bar, and the honour of having the best herbarium and of having been chosen class poet.

On my graduation day an old schoolmate of Father's, who was considered queer because she believed in votes for women, asked him, "George, what career have you selected for this dear girl?"

"The career of a wife and mother," replied Father quickly, with evident disapproval of the question.

The joke of it was that I was educated for neither. I danced, played and sang a little, recited "with so much expression," did fine needlework, painted china and watercolour pictures, made "wonderful" lemon cream pies, angel food, and salad dressing. Because Father made a hobby of mathematics I had been taught geometry, algebra, and trigonometry, which had involved me in the mazes of calculus, logarithms, binomial theorem, permutations, and combinations. I remember nothing about them today except their names. I even had learned to typewrite—a novel accomplishment those days. The school possessed a Remington typewriter, which to me was an ever-fascinating plaything. The Sisters taught us to type our essays, which were on such topics as "Lives of the Prophets," "Greek Philosophers," and "Works of Washington Irving." Father was very proud of mine, and had them bound in red morocco leather. I knew how to dress for and act at receptions, dinner parties, musicales, and dances.

9

I could play tennis and ride, but today I think how little I knew about proper clothes for these sports. For tennis I wore a high-collared starched shirtwaist, long skirt, at least three starched petticoats, and other "unmentionable" undergarments, all belted around my tightly corseted 18-inch waist, a small sailor hat held on the top of my frizzes with two hatpins, long cotton stockings, and high-laced or buttoned boots; for riding, a high silk hat and tailored habit—the skirt gracefully draping the horse as I sat on my side saddle, or sweeping the ground as I walked.

Such a training to prepare me for a wife and mother!

No such thoughts as these, however, troubled me when my graduation day dawned—that beautiful June morning 50 years ago.

The only jarring note for me came with the presentation of the conduct wreaths—gold leaves for the blameless, silver for those not so good, and green for those who just got by. The heads of all the class, save one, were adorned with gold and silver wreaths. I received the green.

However, my chagrin was alleviated considerably on the presentation of bouquets from relatives and admiring friends. I received one which was the most beautiful of all—a dozen calla lilies, the yellow centres removed and each replaced by three tiny tea roses, entwined with maidenhair fern. It was from Will Purdy, my favourite beau.

Chapter II
I AM A YOUNG LADY

Now that my education was finished, I had become a young lady whose chief mission in life was to wait until the right man came along to marry me.

Father, not yet 50 years of age, had established 72 laundries in various parts of the country. He had travelled round the world. He had bought a sugar plantation on the Isle of Pines, one of the West Indies. He was now planning to retire on a 2,000-acre ranch on the border of Kansas and Oklahoma, in the dry belt, the soil of which he hoped to reclaim by a vast irrigation scheme.

While negotiating the purchase of this he took me west with him to visit his sister—my Aunt Ione, wife of John R. Hanna, president of the City National Bank of Denver. She was one of the advanced women of her generation, and later attained the distinction of being the first woman to be elected a member of the Denver School Board.

Susan B. Anthony, the noted woman suffrage pioneer, was also a guest. I recall her as a silver-haired, motherly, pleasant woman, not at all the Carrie Nation window-smashing type. I looked upon her as a super-creature, and had a great shock when I wandered into the sewing room and saw her sewing brush braid on an old black alpaca skirt. I had never dreamed that the great could so descend to the common things of life.

Aunt Ione was a friend of Frances E. Willard, founder of the Women's Christian Temperance Union, who had given up her position as dean of women of the Chicago North-western University to fight for prohibition.

Helen Hunt Jackson and her husband, Dr. Jackson, were frequent visitors at the Hanna home. Helen Hunt was an invalid, and Dr. Jackson generally carried her from their carriage into the house. One of her chief topics of conversation was the injustice of the white men to the Indians, which is the theme of her best-known literary effort, *Ramona*.

Ben Lindsay, who became internationally known as the originator of the juvenile and domestic relations courts, and exponent of companionate marriage, then a very young man, was also an always-welcome guest.

That fall of '85 I was introduced formally to society by Father and Mother at a large evening reception at our home, a spacious 20-room house on Vincennes Avenue on the south side of the city. This was followed by a dance, the carpeted floors of our double drawing-room being covered with canvas.

I was to wear my first evening gown. Father had brought it from Cuba, and it was made of pink surah silk, the tight-fitting laced bodice covered with embroidered pineapple tissue in colour-tones of pink, which was pleated around the decollete neck and fashioned into frills on the three-quarter length sleeves, and three flounces on the wide skirt. I look back on this event as one of the happiest of my life. There was everything to make it so—youth, wealth, pretty clothes—and Will Purdy was there.

It was a gay winter, and I met Will Purdy again and again. He had finished his military education, and was working on the Rock Island Railway in the paymaster's department. Our friendship soon deepened into love, and with the approval of my parents and his father (his mother was dead) we became engaged.

I was now absorbed in preparations for my marriage, which was to take place in the summer. I made many fancywork articles for my "green trunk"—silk-embroidered cushions and centre-pieces, and gros-point coverings for chair seats, stools, and an ottoman. I painted china and watercolours. I ornamented several small pieces of furniture with poker-burning, a so-called pyrographic work. I monogrammed dozens of various articles of table and bed linen.

I was delivered into the hands of dressmakers. I remember some of my prettiest hats and gowns—a black challis, printed with tiny pink roses and green leaves, trimmed with many rows of black lace gathered on with pink ribbon, and a black pancake hat, faced with pink roses; an afternoon frock of fine baby blue lawn enhanced by dozens of yards of Valenciennes lace insertion and small frills, with which I wore a wide leghorn hat trimmed with blue flowers and carried a dainty white silk parasol with blue ribbon bows and streamers. I had two nun's veiling tea gowns with flowing sleeves and long trains, my favourite being one of deep blue, banded with folds of wine-coloured moire silk.

Mother was not well enough to arrange a big wedding, so Will and I were married quietly in August 1887, in the little Memorial Church on the shores of Lake Geneva. I wore a tailored suit of grey silk-warp henrietta cloth, both coat and skirt lined with grey silk. In accordance with the latest fashion of curves and "rustling" I had a stiff grey taffeta silk petticoat and a "five-wire bustle." My matching grey hat was trimmed with a pair of grey wings, and was held in place by two hatpins with large pink knobs which also served as part of the trimming. My high-laced boots and gloves were grey, and I carried a bouquet of pink roses.

We went to Chicago on our honeymoon in father Purdy's private car, and there relatives and friends entertained us royally.

After this we settled down in our suburban home in Walden, 10 miles from Chicago on the Rock Island Railway. The house was Father's gift, and it was completely furnished with wedding presents from relatives on both sides.

Will was now assistant paymaster, and his salary $1,000 a year. In addition he had an expense account, as he had to be away 10 days of each month in the pay car. (Railroad employees those days were paid in cash from a car.) This was sufficient to cover his entire personal expenses, while I had the salary to pay the household bills and the coloured hired girl ($5 a month). Grandfather Munger declared that with such a start we should not only live well, but save money besides.

My first thrill of freedom came with my marriage, when at last, unchaperoned, I could go to the Vienna Bakery, a place with a naughty reputation. I remember my first visit there with two other young matrons, and my deep chagrin when one of my uncles walked in with a blonde. For some reason or other the very word "blonde" conveyed the meaning of "fast woman."

Each day I was through my few household duties quickly and had plenty of time to write bits of verse, which were published sometimes in the Chicago papers and copied by other papers.

Now and again we invited friends to play euchre. Sometimes we took the old "dummy line" and went far out beyond Hyde Park (enormously valuable property now) for a picnic, and I spent pleasant hours looking for wild flowers for a collection which I had started.

My first son, Warren, was born within the year, and I was very happy with my baby. Even today, when I am embarked on a so-called career at the age of 70, if given a choice, I would gladly be the mother of a large family.

Will's greatest friend was Eli Gage, son of Lyman J. Gage, president of the First National Bank, whose name is interwoven in the history of the "windy city" for his expert advice in the financial panic, and later for his philanthropic work.

Will and I accompanied the Gages on the occasion of Eli's marriage to Sophy Weare, sister of the president of the North American Trading and Transportation Company, which had established trading posts in the far north, and operated a fleet of boats on the Yukon River.

It was not very long, but it seemed so then, until Warren was kindergarten age, and I took him every day to Miss Ann Harrison's kindergarten, one of the first to be established in Chicago. My systematic housekeeping allowed plenty of time to stay and help her with the children, as she taught them to weave coloured paper mats, sew perforated cards with coloured wool, and play children's games.

This pleasant work was discontinued because of the birth of my second son, Donald. Like all mothers of small children I was engrossed in the work and care that goes with motherhood. But soon (too soon, I say now) my boys were in school. Will was promoted to the position of paymaster; we were better off; I did not have enough to do at home, and I looked for outside interests. Chicago was booming. My immediate relatives were making money hand over fist, and I was soon caught up in a whirl of life outside my home.

It was in the beginning of the '90's that men and women leaders of the local "Four Hundred," business and political circles mooted the idea of the World's Fair, to be held in Chicago. It opened in 1893. Mrs. Potter Palmer, president of the "Board of Lady Managers," and her sister, Mrs. Fred Grant, known as "the beautiful Honore girls," were close friends of Aunt Martha Morse, and for that reason I was included in many social and other affairs which revolved around them during the fair. I became a glorified errand girl for Mrs. Potter Palmer, whom I so admired, and delighted to be at her beck and call. I was present at the dedication services when she opened the Women's Building, driving a golden nail with a silver hammer. She chose me as one of the attendants upon Lady Aberdeen, wife of the Earl of Aberdeen, who later became Governor-General of Canada. Lady Aberdeen had been instrumental in raising funds for the Irish building, and had come over specially to open it.

I was at the fair that July day when the cold storage warehouse caught fire, and 15 firemen were trapped in the tallest of the three towers. I can still hear the groans and shrieks of that huge crowd watching those brave men face silently the horrible death of being burned alive.

Our family was particularly saddened the last day of the fair by the assassination of Carter Harrison, Chicago's grand old "booster mayor," who was a warm friend of father Purdy's.

After the World's Fair there followed a period known as hard times. Factories closed, stores ran with greatly reduced staffs, and hundreds of breadwinners were out of work. The city organized relief schemes on a huge scale, but in spite of that it was a winter of misery, expecially for women and children.

With other young women I helped Jane Addams at Hull House. This famous social worker had come to Chicago in 1889, and with Ellen Gates Starr had leased a house, owned by a man named Hull, and made it their headquarters. I saw so many heart-rending sights—hungry, homeless families; small thinly dressed children picking coal on the railway tracks, which were not fenced as they are today. I worked hard to collect food and clothing for the needy, money to buy coal, which in the bitter weather, was as essential as and certainly more costly than food.

While I did not suffer personal privation, our family was directly affected by the railway strikes, which revolved about Eugene Debs, who was promoting the organization of railway employees into "One Big Union." We had many anxious hours over paralysed railway traffic—burning of millions of dollars of railway equipment—shooting in railway yards—city under martial law—carloads of troops—and finally the explosion on Michigan Avenue, which shook that part of the city for blocks. Some said it was an explosion of an ammunition wagon, and others that it was a bomb. Needless to say the very name Debs was anathema in our family.

But I had my share of the gaiety of the gay '90's too. The bicycle built for two became the rage. Father Purdy gave us a tandem and, with nine other young married couples, we formed a cycling club. What fun we had! We rode round the parks and took picnic lunches, or met at the German Building, one of the few left from the fair. We had progressive dinners of six and eight courses, one course to a home.

There were no afternoon tea-parties, but I was "at home" the last Thursday of the month, prepared to serve my callers hot chocolate with whipped cream, sandwiches, and cake. After the World's Fair, chocolate gave way to tea. Instead of bridge following our luncheons, we played euchre or went to a matinee. Dinners were very formal, and other evening functions took the form of soirees in honour of distinguished guests, progressive euchre or pedro parties, socials, when we played charades and other guessing games, musicales, theatre box parties followed by suppers, and house dances. Another popular diversion of our set was to gather at the Palmer House, have Turkish baths, meet our husbands for lunch, and go to the matinee.

Then there were the high never-to-be-forgotten performances of the great Shakespearian actors and actresses—Sir Henry Irving and Ellen Terry, Edward Sothern and Julia Marlowe, Lawrence Barrett, and others; the lighter moments of the modern dramas, musical comedies, and revues, which starred Lillian Russell, Nat Goodwin, Joe Jefferson, and the Haverly Minstrels. And could I forget Sousa (and wasn't he handsome?), or the glorious music of his band, and the Theodore Thomas orchestra in the old Central Music Hall, which was later torn down to make way for the new part of Marshall Field?

The Cuban Rebellion of 1895 drew me into my first women's club work. At that time in United States sympathy for Cuba's liberty and her oppressed people ran high. Public opinion was inflamed by the Hearst papers, with stories of terrible treatment and persecution by the Spaniards and propaganda that the States should make Cuba's liberty an issue with Spain. This finally resulted in the Spanish-American War of 1898.

Today I would not be so biased or moved by the stories or cruelties of one faction in any war. Each opposing party can match story for story—as my father and mother did in the Civil War. All wars bring out the most bestial qualities in men, for the lust to kill is only aroused by fanning the fires of hatred—and what better fuel is there for this than the usual war-atrocity stories?

It was at a reception in the fall of 1897 that I met the great East Indian palmist, Count de Hamong, famed as "Cheiro." His secretary came to me and, bowing low, said, "My master craves the honour of an audience with you." Excited and flattered at being picked out, I readily consented and we made the appointment for next morning.

On arrival I was ushered into a dimly lighted room where Cheiro, dressed in flowing purple robes, was seated at a table. Before him, resting on a purple velvet cushion, was a long golden serpent, with ruby eyes and a flat emerald head, used later to trace the lines of my hand.

Quickly he read my left hand, calling it the hand I "was born with." The lines showed two marriages, several children, but a long life.

As I stretched out my right hand it seemed to me that the red eyes of the golden serpent, moving over the lines of my palm, gleamed wickedly, the emerald head shone with a deeper brilliancy. Then Cheiro said slowly:

"You are leaving this country within the year. You will travel far. You will face danger, privation, and sorrow. Although you are going to a foreign land you will be among English-speaking people, and will never have to learn to speak another language. You will have another child, a girl, or an unusually devoted son."

I listened, scoffing in my heart. But the next summer my home was broken up. Will and I had parted forever. I was speeding northward to the Klondyke, where, that winter, all alone in a little cabin of that grim north country, I was to face the darkest hours of my life—the birth of my youngest son, Lyman. ⟫✖⟪

Chapter III
THE GOLD FEVER

Gold in the Klondyke! . . . gold by the ton . . . gold, grains the size of rice, by the bucketful . . . gold, nuggets as large as hens' eggs . . . gold, from the grass roots, for the panning! That was the news flashed round the world in 1897.

The discovery had been made the year before on Bonanza Creek, but word of it spread slowly among the few pioneers scattered over that vast northern wilderness. There was no up-river steamer, no telegraph, no regular mail service. The only means of communication was by "moccasin telegraph" (word of mouth) or the odd letter carried by Indians or the very occasional traveller, who had to mush on for days through snow-filled valleys, over frozen rivers and mountain passes in winter, or travel thousands of miles of waterways by canoe, scow, or poling boat in summer. Months had passed before that ever-alluring cry of "gold" reached the outside world, where it precipitated one of the maddest gold rushes in history.

In the autumn of '97 a few got through, but in the spring of '98, as soon as the ice was running in the Yukon River, there was a stampede of gold seekers. Thousands came from all parts of the globe—men of all races and nationalties, crafts, and professions, the majority having no more knowledge of mining than the man in the moon.

The gold fever hit Chicago. Will, tired of his paymaster's job, and his friend, Eli Gage, who worked in his father's bank, made plans to join the rush. Backed by their respective fathers, they formed the Purdy-Gage Company, which purchased two ocean-going tugs, one steamer, and two sailing vessels.

The more they talked about the trip the more I wanted to go. It looked like a great adventure, and I was consumed with the urge to have my part in it. I had been married 10 years. Will was away from home most of the time, and I was unhappy. Both boys were well started at school. Father and Mother offered to care for them at Catalpa Knob, their Kansas ranch. Eli's wife, Sophy, also wanted to go. Father Purdy and Mr. Gage talked it over, and agreed it might be well for us wives to accompany our husbands.

Then one day a strange incident occurred, this being the real factor in the final decision concerning my going. A man by the name of Lambert, an employee of the Rock Island Railway, hearing that Will was going to the Klondyke, came up from Kansas City to tell father Purdy a remarkable story. He said that an uncle of his, one William Lambert, had died in the Klondyke and willed to the family a million dollars in gold dust, already mined, and marvellously rich properties. He had in his possession a copy of this will, which he showed father Purdy. He wondered if Will would look into it and act as the family's agent.

Father Purdy suggested that this be my special work. The idea was acceptable to all concerned, and the proper papers were drawn up. Father Purdy insisted that I should receive a 50 per cent division of the gold dust, half a million dollars, and if I did not survive this hazardous undertaking, that it should be made over to my children.

To me it was a quest that had all the allure of a "Treasure Island" or "Aladdin's Lamp." I had only to go to the world-famed goldfields, lay before the Canadian authorities proof that I was the family's agent, and collect the gold. I pictured myself and children living in luxury the rest of our days. I look back now and wonder how anyone could have been taken in, as I was; could have been persuaded to go on such a wild goose chase; and that men with years of business experience—a railway president and a great banker—could have thought that such a huge fortune was to be had merely for the taking.

I took the boys to Catalpa Knob, where my brother George and my cousin, Harry Peachey, so caught my enthusiasm that they decided to join the party. After a few wavering moments, which always come to mothers when parting with their little ones, and with my heart full of gratitude to Father and Mother, who had been unusually sympathetic, I, with George and Harry, left to meet Will and the Gages in Denver.

In this city we outfitted ourselves completely with clothes for the trip. I recall purchasing a plentiful supply of Jaeger "combinations," merino stockings, high boots of Russian leather with elkhide soles (these later proving a godsend in securing footholds on the slippery, slushy trail), a natty straw sailor hat which my brother carried over the Chilkoot Pass on the end of a stick as it could not be packed, and the last word in an outing costume of the late '90's. This was made of heavily ribbed tobacco-brown corduroy velvet with a skirt of shockingly immodest length (it actually showed my ankles), five yards around the bottom, edged with brush braid, and lined with brown silk and interlined with a foot of buckram, which gave it a fetching swing as I walked. It had a Norfolk jacket with many pleats, a blouse with a high stiff collar almost to my ears, and a pair of voluminous brown silk bloomers, which came below the knee.

We then continued gaily to Seattle, where we were joined by Captain Spencer, the business agent for the Purdy-Gage Company, his son Ed, and Captain Treat. Our plans were that Eli and Sophy, his wife, should go to San Francisco, and from there to St. Michaels, headquarters of the Yukon Trading and Transportation Company, of which Sophy's brother, P. B. Weare, was president, whence they would go up the Yukon River to Dawson. The rest of the party was to take the boat at Seattle, go to Skagway, walk over the Chilkoot or Chilkat Pass, and thence by the Yukon waterway to Dawson.

We had been in Seattle only a few days when Will was called to San Francisco by a telegram from the Gages on what appeared to be a hurried final business consultation. Little did I know at the time that this telegram was to change my whole life. Within a week he wrote he would be delayed in 'Frisco—he didn't know exactly how long. He wrote again that he had changed his mind about going to the Klondyke—he'd heard such terrible stories of the hardships of the trail. He had heard, too, that great fortunes were being made in the Sandwich Islands (now the Hawaiian Islands). Would I consider going there? Or perhaps I had better go home to my people until he made up his mind what to do.

Go to the Sandwich Islands? With my Klondyke ticket bought, my passage booked, my vision of a million dollars in gold dust? Even after 10 years of married life how little Will Purdy knew me!

Now I realize that this was more than just my headstrong determination to carry out an idea. It was the pivotal point of my life—my destiny. The North Star, my lodestar, beckoned me. It lured me onward. My whole being cried out to follow it. Miserable and heartbroken as I was, I could not turn back.

At first my brother sided with Will. He refused flatly to take any responsibility for my going without my husband. He threatened to send for Father to *make* me go home. I coaxed, pleaded, cajoled. I said I would go alone. I was tired of the monotonous round of the society life of Chicago . . . of the loneliness of the days on end when Will had been away on his paymaster's job. . . . This was my opportunity to seek and claim my fortune. . . . I'd never ask a thing of him again. . . . George gave in—and promised that not until we were well on our way would he let Father know what had happened.

It would serve no purpose to tell the details of this tragedy in my life. It was so long ago—one thing had led to another, and this was the crisis which parted two high-spirited and determined young people. I wrote to Will that I had made up my mind to go to the Klondyke as originally planned, that I would never go back to him, so undependable he had proven, that I never wanted to hear from or see him again. He went his way. I went mine. I never did see Will Purdy again. He died years later in Honolulu.

The Gages went to Eagle, Alaska, where Eli was taken sick and they turned back. The Purdy-Gage Company was short-lived, and the boats were sold to Sophy's brother's company, the North American Trading and Transportation.

Utterly engrossed as I was in my personal troubles, I do not remember much of Seattle that June of '98, except its waterfront. Over its wharves surged jostling eager crowds of miners, prospectors, traders, trappers, and adventurers, all dressed in the clothes of the trail—hideous red-and-yellow plaid mackinaws, overalls tucked into high boots, and caps of all descriptions. Everywhere were piles of outfits—camp supplies, sleds, carts, harness, which, together with dogs, horses, cattle, and oxen, were being loaded into various boats, sailing almost every hour. These, too, were of all descriptions—steamers, sailing vessels, dories manned by stout hands—all to leave, some never to be seen or heard of again, others to be dashed upon the rocks of the bleak shore by the cruel waves of the Inside Passage.

Our party of six engaged passage on a small coast steamer which had been laid up for several seasons, but was due to sail on June 23. She was most unattractive-looking, but said to be thoroughly seaworthy (which was something those days), and we were assured that her captain knew the Inside Passage. She was called the *Utopia*, but one wag described her as "The Tadly-adly, Queen Anne front, Mary Anne behind, two decks, and no bottom."

21

Single berths to Skagway cost $50; double $75. In order that I might travel comfortably, a stateroom with three berths had been booked for me at a cost of $120. When I arrived I saw other bags in it, and presumed that it was a mistake. I was soon told, to my shocked surprise, that I was to have company. The double lower had been allotted to a tinhorn gambler and his female companion, the middle to me, and the upper to "Birdie," destined to be one of the most notorious characters of the Klondyke. My brother George and I protested to the captain and purser; but we realized very quickly that we were in a hopeless minority. In the language of today, "We could take it or leave it." The only concession allowed me was the choice of the time to get up and go to bed.

The steamer was certainly a has-been. She was dirty, and loaded to the gunwales with passengers, animals, and freight. Men slept on the floor of the saloon and in every corner. The captain was seldom, if ever, sober, and there were many wild parties. Poker, blackjack, and drinking went on night and day, and our safe arrival in Skagway was due probably to the Guiding Hand that looks after children, fools, and drunken men.

After a day out everyone became accustomed to his unusual surroundings, the weather was perfect, the meals were fairly well cooked and served, and a spirit of optimism prevailed as time flew by on the wings of novelty. I became accustomed to my stateroom companions; their kindness soothed my outraged feelings. Every morning the gambler brought me coffee, and I heard his bedfellow tell him, "You see that her toast is thin, you know she has a delikat stummick." Birdie, too, often gave me an orange or apple from her supplies. No longer did I weep in secret at our strange sleeping arrangements.

It took seven days to make that thousand miles of sea voyage, only one day and a half in the open, and the remainder in the Inside Passage, winding between the coast islands. After the first two days there was no darkness, only a few hours of twilight, which, as we journeyed north, became paler until, upon our arrival at Skagway, it was continuous light.

We arrived at Skagway at 11 o'clock at night. As we docked, a dozen newsboys jumped aboard immediately for huge bundles of newspapers, which sold like hot cakes at "four bits" apiece. Of all that motley crowd which met the boat two figures are clearly etched in my mind: One, a beautiful painted woman, in a much be-ruffled princess dress and a huge be-feathered and be-flowered merry widow hat, lolling in a hack, who called "Hallo!" to the captain; the other, a fine figure of a man with heavy flowing black moustaches, mounted on a white horse, which came clattering down the plank wharf. I never learned the name of the former, who was evidently a "lily of the field," but the name of the other was hurriedly whispered from person to person. It was Soapy Smith, the bold bad man of the North, now cited as one of the most notorious villains the North has ever known.

The infamous Soapy came to his end 10 days after our arrival. Meeting the *Utopia* was evidently one of his last public appearances. After his death it was easy to roundup the members of his gang, who were either imprisoned or told to "Mush on!"*

After a day or so of unloading at Skagway—miners' outfits, rails for the new road which was being built through the White Pass, horses (the majority soon to be killed on the trail), and cattle—the *Utopia* puffed slowly to Dyea, the small, ever-changing town of tents, just around the bend of the Lynn Canal, within a few miles of the towering Chilkoot Pass. Our outfit was dumped on the sandy shore and the little steamer pulled away on her return. As I watched her depart I realized that I had burned my bridges behind me, that I had left civilization, with its comforts and luxuries.

I was not overcome with loneliness or fright as I looked directly before me at the fearful mountain pass that was to go down in history as "the worst trail this side of hell." I thought of my New England forebears, women who had bravely faced the hardships of pioneering, coupled with the constant fear of attacking Indians; of my great-great-Aunt Sophia, who, with a babe at her breast, had driven with her husband across a blazing, wind-swept prairie. I thought of Mother, how nobly she had met the adversities of life. Once again I knew that my path lay ahead, that there was no turning aback now.

While looking about Dyea to find a place to pitch our tents, Captain Spencer became acquainted with a young man who most generously placed his rough board shack at my disposal, while he, the owner, bunked with a friend next door. It was a small one-room shanty, 12 by 14 feet, furnished with a sheet-iron cookstove, two chairs, and a table. It had a built-in narrow bunk and some

*A corruption of the French word *marchons*.

packing-box cupboards. The men set up tents for their sleeping-quarters, and we lived here pleasantly for a fortnight.

George, travelling light, walked over the Chilkoot and White Pass to find out which was easier, but having since been over both, I am convinced that there was no choice, that, if anything, the Chilkoot was the harder. We spent our time fishing, climbing mountain paths to limber up for the trip ahead, and I whiled away many a happy hour picking wild flowers. For the first time in my life I saw hillsides of wild blue iris and lupine, or blue bonnet, now the official flower of Texas. It had indeed wandered far from home.

I was chief cook and bottle-washer, but this work was simplified by a limited diet, and the dish-washing minimized, as we carried the fewest of granite dishes and cooking utensils. One morning, after I had finished the breakfast dishes, George said, "Now, Polly (that was his nickname for me), let me have the dishpan. I want to wash my socks." I objected strenuously. "Well, you needn't get so huffy about it. I took a bath in it last night." And so one of my first lessons of life in the North was to adjust myself to the fact that one and the same pan must serve the purpose of dishpan, bread-mixer, bath, and washtub. Many times I exclaimed, "Thank heaven we have plenty of Ivory soap and Sapolio!"

The time came very soon for us to leave Dyea, this last outpost of civilization, and we celebrated the evening before by having an oyster stew, at fairly reasonable prices—oysters $1.50 a quart, and fresh milk $1 a gallon.　　　　　　　　　　　　　　　　　　➤✳❮

Chapter IV
THE TRAIL OF '98

We left Dyea on July 12 at noon, to walk the dreaded trail of 42 miles over the Chilkoot Pass to Lake Bennett, first to Sheep Camp at the foot of the Pass, then to the summit, down to Lake Lindeman, round the shores of that beautiful lake, past the rapids and finally to the little village of Bennett.

With staff in hand, at last I had taken my place in that continuous line of pushing humans and straining animals. Before me, behind me, abreast of me almost every man toted a pack of 60 to 80 pounds, in addition to driving dogs and horses harnessed to sleighs and carts, herding pack ponies and the odd cow, while one woman drove an ox-cart.

We were lucky enough to be travelling light. We had let out a contract to a company of packers for the transportation of our clothing, bedding, and "grub," which weighed several tons. After much haggling we had secured a "reduced" price of $900 spot cash—this, in the words of the packers, "a damn low figger." After I got over the Pass I agreed; it was a super-human effort to transport those thousands of pounds up that narrow, slippery, rocky trail of the Pass, through boulder-strewn canyons, across swampy bottomlands. It meant changing every box and bundle from steamer to wagon, to horse, to man, to sled, and finally to horse, before they were landed on the shores of Lake Bennett, where we were to wait for the building of our boat, which was to take us downriver to Dawson.

A quarter of a mile from Dyea we crossed a toll bridge, and after the attendant had collected our toll of $1 each, he abused us because we would not buy a $5 steering paddle to use on the lakes and rivers on the other side of the Pass. Fancy paying this price for it and carrying it over the trail too!

For five or six miles we followed a good wagon road, through cool, shady woods. We forded several clear mountain streams by stepping from stone to stone, and now and then I was carried across pick-a-back. (I weighed only 110 pounds those days.) The trail became rockier, and we scrambled over tons of enormous stones and boulders, through four miles of a valley, with hardly a tuft of vegetation. It might have been the playground of the gods, so wild it seemed! My bulky clothes made the walking hard. My pity went out to the beasts of burden carrying their heavy loads. At three o'clock we stopped a half-hour for refreshments at a wayside cabin, kept by a widow and her little son. She brewed us a cup of strong tea, and as we ate substantial ham sandwiches, told us gruelling stories of the rush of the year before.

Refreshed and undaunted we continued, soon reaching the little settlement of Canyon City. Here we struck the mountain trail which led to Sheep Camp, at the foot of the Pass, where we planned to spend the night. As we travelled we began to realize that we were indeed on a trail of heartbreaks and dead hopes. On every side were mute evidences—scores of dead horses that had slipped and fallen down the mountainside (so few got over the Pass), and caches of miners' outfits. We looked into a deserted shanty, where lay a mildewed ruined outfit. "Home of two brothers who died from exposure last winter," they told us.

And was I glad to call it a day when we arrived at Sheep Camp, the small shack and tent village of one street huddled between precipitous mountains. There seemed nothing permanent about it save the isolated glacier that glittered and sparkled in the sun above our heads. Before us was a huge pile of snow, ice, and rocks, the debris of the snowslide which had happened at Easter, and had crushed to death 30 such adventurers as we. We were greeted with the news that several more bodies had been discovered that day. They were buried under a large cairn of stones which was pointed out to every newcomer. As I looked at it I could not help but feel that such a sudden end—to be snuffed out without a chance to make one's peace with one's Maker, and in a mad search for gold—was surely an ignominious death.

I looked up the Pass. I can see it yet—that upward trail, outlined on an almost perpendicular wall of ice-covered rock, alive with clinging human beings and animals, slowly mounting, single file, to the summit.

We stopped at the Grand Pacific Hotel. In writing home a description of this to Father and Mother, I said, "Look at your woodshed. Fit it up with 'standees,' and you have the Grand

Pacific." But I had no such uppish attitude when, weary and footsore, I staggered in, and when I left, my heart was warm with gratitude to the elderly couple who kept it. In addition to the regular supper bill of fare I had half a canned peach. I was given the only "private room" in the house—a cubicle partitioned off by a wooden wall, two-thirds the height of the room, with a built-in bunk filled with hay and covered with two pairs of grey army blankets—and comfort of comforts!—a real feather pillow!

After a wonderful night's sleep, a hearty breakfast of corn meal mush, bacon and cold-storage eggs, condensed milk, prunes, and a whole orange—the last in the camp—and settling our hotel bill (meals and bunk $1 apiece), with high hearts that glorious July morning we started to climb that 3,000 feet of steep, narrow, icy mountain trail. The Indians said there was a curse on all who attempted it in summer, as the hot sun melted the winter snow, and it came crashing down—crushing everything before it. These avalanches had already taken toll of nearly 100 lives.

For the first hour we walked over the trail of the recent slide. In the melting snow I saw a bit of blue ribbon. Bending down, I

Sheep Camp offered the last firewood and shelter to be found west of the summit. No wonder Martha found her long skirt a serious hindrance!

27

tugged at it and pulled out a baby's bootee. Did it belong to some venturesome soul who had come to seek a fortune for wife and baby? Would those who were waiting for him wait in vain? Was this one of the hundreds of tragedies of this mad stampede?

I did not dare look round at the magnificent mountain scenery nor drink in the beauty of the tumbling torrents, for every minute the melting snow was making it more slippery under foot. The greatest of care was needed in crossing the dangerously thin ice that was often the only bridge over a mountain stream, which had paused a few moments on a narrow ledge, to drop over a precipice, hundreds of feet below.

As the day advanced the trail became steeper, the air warmer, and footholds without support impossible. I shed my sealskin jacket. I cursed my hot, high, buckram collar, my tight heavily boned corsets, my long corduroy skirt, my full bloomers which I had to hitch up with every step. We clung to stunted pines, spruce roots, jutting rocks. In some places the path was so narrow that, to move at all, we had to use our feet tandem fashion. Above, only the granite walls. Below, death leering at us.

But soon, too soon, I was straining every nerve, every ounce of physical endurance in that ever upward climb. There were moments when, with sweating forehead, pounding heart, and panting breath, I felt I could go no farther. At such times we dropped out of line and rested in the little snow dug-outs along the way. But such a few moments of rest! Then on with that cursing procession of men and dogs and horses, pulling sleds or toting packs.

Mush on . . . Mush on . . . It beat into my brain. . . . Cracking of whips. . . .Wild screams of too heavily loaded pack horses which lost their footing and were dashed to the rocks below . . . stumbling . . . staggering . . . crawling. . . . God pity me!

Mush on . . . Mush on. . . . Another breath! Another step. . . . God give me strength. How far away that summit! Can I ever make it?

Mush on . . . Mush on . . . or die!

"Cheer up, cheer up, Polly!" I hear George break the long silence. "Only a hundred feet to go now." One hundred feet! That sheer wall of rock! Can I make it? In some inexplicable way the men of our party get round me. They push and pull me. They turn and twist me, until my very joints creak with the pain of it. "Don't look down," they warn. I have no strength to turn my head, to speak. Only 10 feet more! Oh, God, what a relief!

Then my foot slips! I lose my balance. I fall only a few feet into a crevice in the rocks. The sharp edge of one cuts through my boot and I feel the flesh of my leg throbbing with pain. I can bear it no longer, and I sit down and do what every woman does in time of stress. I weep. "Can I help you?" "Can I help you?" asks every man who passes me. George tries to comfort me but in vain. He becomes impatient. "For God's sake, Polly, buck up and be a man! Have some style and move on!"

Was I mad? Not even allowed the comfort of tears! I bucked up all right and walked triumphantly into that broker's tent—an ancient canvas structure on the summit. I had made the top of the world, but "the wind that blew between the spheres" cut me like a knife. I was tired, faint, hungry, cold. I asked for a fire, and was answered, "Madame, wood is two bits a pound up here." George, who was really concerned about me, spoke up: "All right. All right. I'll be a sport. Give her a $5 fire." One heavenly hour of rest. I took off my boots, washed my wounded shin and poured iodine on it. I dried my wet stockings, had a cup of tea, and got thoroughly warm.

We then went through customs, as we had now entered Canada. Around us, shivering in the cold wind, were many waiting people, their outfits partially unpacked and scattered about them in the deep snow. It was here that I met for the first time members of the North West Mounted Police, and I thought that finer, sturdier, more intelligent-looking men would be hard to find.

Then the descent! Down, ever downward. Weight of body on shaky legs, weight growing heavier, and legs shakier. Sharp rocks to scratch our clutching hands. Snake-like roots to trip our stumbling feet.

We stopped at the half-way cabin for a $2 supper of bean soup, ham and eggs (of uncertain age), prunes, bread, and butter—the bread served with the apology of the proprietor, "The middle of it ain't done, but you don't have to eat it. I hurried too much."

I had felt that I could make no greater effort in my life than the last part of the upward climb, but the last two miles into Lindeman was the most excruciating struggle of the whole trip. In my memory it will ever remain a hideous nightmare. The trail led through a scrub pine forest where we tripped over bare roots of trees that curled over and around rocks and boulders like great devilfishes.

29

Rocks! Rocks! Rocks! Tearing boots to pieces. Hands bleeding with scratches. I can bear it no longer. In my agony I beg the men to leave me—to let me lie in my tracks, and stay for the night.

My brother put his arm around me and carried me most of the last mile. Captain Spencer hurried into the village, to the Tacoma Hotel, to get a bed for me. It wasn't much of a bed either—a canvas stretched on four logs, with a straw shakedown, yet the downiest couch in the world or the softest bed in a king's palace could not have made a better resting-place for me.

As my senses slipped away into the unconsciousness of that deep sleep of exhaustion, there surged through me a thrill of satisfaction. I had actually walked over the Chilkoot Pass! . . . I would never do it again, knowing now what it meant. . . . Not for all the gold in the Klondyke. . . . And yet, knowing now what it meant, would I miss it? . . . No, never! . . . Not even for all the gold in the world!

George Merrick Munger, Martha's young brother, with whom she climbed the Chilkoot Trail in 1898, who encouraged her through the tough parts and saw her through the birth of her Little Cheechako in the log cabin at Dawson City.

Chapter V

LAKE BENNETT TO DAWSON

Feeling the effects of our Herculean efforts of the day before, we rested long in the canvas camp at Lindeman. My energy was so drained that I spent most of the time on my cot or sitting on moss-covered rocks looking at a cloudless sky, reflected in the rippling waters of the lake, after which the camp was named. By evening I was ready to go on, and the party decided to walk the two miles to Lake Bennett, where we hoped our baggage had arrived, as planned, and set up our camp for the night. But in this we were disappointed, although the packers had assured us it would be there "as soon as you are."

There were two or three so-called hotels, canvas-roofed, wooden affairs, each of which had kitchen, dining room, bar, and dance hall—all in the one room. The walls were lined with bunks on two sides—but they were all taken. It was impossible to find a bed for me. One man casually offered to share his bunk with me. Finally a good-natured packer, taking pity on me, told George that we might sleep under some canvas-covered hay. "But don't you scatter that hay about. It's worth $250 a ton," he warned. Fortunately the weather was mild, and for several nights our party—five men and one woman—was glad of these somewhat crowded sleeping-quarters. And still our outfit had not arrived! Vainly we searched that crowded town of Bennett for a tent, shack, or cabin, but the whole world seemed to be waiting for the building of boats to speed it down to Dawson.

We heard of two cabins back at Lindeman, above the rapids connecting the two lakes, and we walked back. They were owned by a party of Australians, who gave us the cabins they were just leaving, telling us to pass them on to someone else when we were through.

Then followed two weeks of as wonderful a camping experience as I have ever had. The camp site commanded a magnificent view of snow-capped peaks, ranged round in fanlike folds about the limpid lake. The weather was perfect. Shortly after midnight the sun rose, revolved in spiral fashion, mounted higher and higher till it reached the zenith at noon, then sank lower and lower until it dipped below the horizon. Daytime and night-time merged into each other so softly, so imperceptibly, that we scarcely realized the change.

It was here I learned to make sourdough, which, in the early days of the Klondyke, took the place of yeast, which could not be had in the country. This is the recipe:

> Mix a thin batter of flour and water. Add a little rice water or macaroni water and a pinch of sugar. Put mixture in a pail, cover it, and hang over the stove, keeping it warm for four hours. Sourdough may be used to raise bread, pancakes, and doughnuts. For pancakes use a pinch of soda.

Even today I can make sourdough pancakes that will melt in your mouth.

This, too, is the origin of the name "sourdough," meaning pioneers of '98 or before. Today newcomers claim they are sourdoughs if they have seen the ice form in the rivers in the fall and go out in the spring, but they are "chechakos," the Indian word for "newcomer" or "do nothing."

Sometimes the men went hunting, and many a blue grouse they got. I was supposed to have full charge of the cooking, but more often than not one of the party took the job off my hands, leaving only the pies, pancakes, and doughnuts to me.

I had plenty of time to explore the country around. On the higher hills I found quantities of dainty mountain forget-me-nots, growing cheek by jowl with the pink snake weed, the mountain harebell, and the brilliant cerise shooting stars. Lower down were saucy Dutchmen's breeches, bleeding heart (a prototype of the kind that grew in grandmother Munger's garden), exquisite in their waxen beauty, the single, heart-shaped blossoms giving forth an almost intoxicating fragrance, and the tiny twin flowers or Linnaea, the favourite of Linnaeus, the Swedish "father of botany." Sometimes I watched the northern cannibal, the sundew (a distant relative of the Venus flytrap), at work during the drowsy summer days, literally sucking the life fluid of countless unwary midges trapped on the sticky hairy-coated thick leaves. I've actually seen the leaves bloat during this banquet.

Often I walked to Bennett, to the little pioneer church which was being built at the head of the lake—a symbol of man's homage to our Creator, whose power and glory were so evident in the magnificent world around me.

Every night the campers gathered about the enormous fireplace in the large cabin, which my brother George and I had taken for ourselves, and we did enjoy its warmth and cheer in the cool mountain air. When our baggage finally arrived we unpacked George's mandolin and my guitar, and had a sing-song. We sang "The Bicycle Built for Two" and "The Man on the Flying Trapeze," popular songs of the day, and followed these with many old favourites and hymns. Then, deliciously tired from the day in the open, and sleepy from the bracing air, we retired to rest on fragrant pine boughs, piled high on our bunks or on the ground.

One morning we discovered that a bear had visited our camp. It had stolen part of a ham hanging on one of the outside rafters of the cabin and slobbered over a tin of butter in a vain attempt to get at it. For many nights one or another of the men sat up to catch him, but with no luck. In the meantime I insisted that I have a loaded gun by my bunk, much to the amusement of the men, who said if there was a chance for me to use it I would likely point the wrong end.

One night I was aroused by a stealthy-creeping rustling noise. I got up quickly, put on my slippers, grabbed my gun, and ran across the dirt floor.

"Polly, Polly, get back in bed!" called my brother.

With a subdued "Shut up!" I crept to the window, raised my hand to remove the canvas screen, and let out a piercing shriek. Up my sleeve and out of the back of my gown was running the animal that I feared most of all in the world—a mouse. Did I voice that fear too—with shriek after shriek, arousing the whole camp! For days it was the standing joke. One old-timer, looked me over speculatively, saying, as he chewed his wad of tobacco, "Walked over the Pass. Goin' through the rapids. Campin' a long ways from home. Pretty rough life. Ain't afraid of nuthin' but a mouse. Lordy! Wimmin is queer."

One afternoon I was standing on the shore of Lake Bennett, watching the little group around the *Flora*, the first of the river steamboats to attempt the passage of Miles Canyon and the White Horse Rapids, when I saw a new woman, different from the usual type coming into the country. She was wearing a smart-looking raincape and a tweed hat, and, as she turned, I noted that she was not so pretty as clever-looking. I walked over and introduced myself. She told me her name, Flora Shaw, and that she had been sent to the Klondyke by the London *Times*, of which she was the colonial editor. She had allowed a month's time to make the trip from London, England, to Dawson, but it was taking her much longer than that. She asked me where I lived and I replied, "Chicago—but I have lately come from Kansas, where my father owns a large ranch."

"Do you know my brother? He lives in Eureka, Kansas." I did, as this was the nearest post office to Catalpa Knob, which proves, as has been done so often, that the world is really small. I met her again in London in wartime, she, in the meantime, having married Lord Lugard, a colonial governor.

In three weeks our boat was finished. She was a fine unpainted craft, shaped like a fisherman's dory and built of Alaska pine at King's shipyard, Lake Bennett, at a cost of $275. She was 37 feet long, 6½ feet across the bottom, and 8½ feet at the top.

In a short time our goods were loaded. When our several tons of luggage and our party of six got in, there was very little space above the water-line and very little room inside. However, we sailed away in a drenching rain, before a high wind, followed by the gaze of an admiring and curious crowd. As we were well protected by our oil-skins we did not mind the rain, although we were a bit cramped.

By evening we had reached the lower end of Lake Bennett at Caribou Crossing (now Carcross), a distance of 40 miles, and there pitched camp. I had my first experience of cooking supper for five hungry men over a smoky campfire built of wet wood, but we were fortunate in having with us boiled ham, corn meal mush for frying, and plenty of bread.

The next morning dawned clear and beautiful, and we were well under way by six o'clock. With two blanket-sails spread we rushed along at a rapid rate, into a narrow strip of water called Windy Arm, rightly named, as we were forced to land twice on the lee shore because of high winds. Then into Lake Tagish, at the foot of which was a log North West Mounted Police post, in front of some tall evergreens.

Here all boats were stopped and overhauled in a search for liquor. I did not notice until later how solicitous the men of our party were for my comfort. They insisted that I sit on a couple of boxes covered with blankets and a fur robe. Afterwards I found out that these boxes contained two cases of Scotch whisky.

The young officer in charge of the post was fine-looking, well dressed, and exceedingly polite to me. I admired the handsome buttons of his uniform, and he asked me it I would accept one for a hatpin—he had sent some home to his sisters for that purpose. I was delighted, for it would certainly be a unusual souvenir to show when I got home. He told me of a man who was ill in a near-by cabin, and I went over to see him and left several jars of beef tea, which won his extreme gratitude as this could not be had for love or money.

When we left, the young officer told me that since the previous May 18,000 men had passed the post and I was the 631st woman. He numbered our boat 14,405.

We reached Lake Marsh, which pours into the narrow river that rushes through Miles Canyon with its massive, forbidding walls of granite. Many were fearful of our heavily loaded boat attempting it. There was said to be a $100 fine levied on the owner of any boat taking a woman through the canyon and the White Horse Rapids below. But rather than walk that five miles of portage alone, I chose to go by our boat, which was to be piloted by Captain Spencer, an experienced navigator.

We sped through the canyon. There was a breath-taking interval before we were swept into the seething cauldron of the White Horse Rapids, where so many venturesome souls had lost their lives and outfits. Half-way through our steering oar broke with a crack like that of a pistol shot, above the roaring waters. For a tense moment the boat whirled half her length about in the current. Captain Spencer quickly seized another oar, calling coolly, "Never mind, boys! Let her go stern to." A second's hesitation and our lives would have paid the penalty. It took the boat only 26 minutes to get through.

Below the rapids lay Whitehorse, another small tented town, a haven of rest to us. Did I say rest? I spoke too soon, for I had forgotten the pestiferous mosquito, with its needle-like sting and its voracious appetite. We swathed ourselves in mosquito netting, rubbed eucalyptus oil on our hands and faces, but then the

Freight is unloaded at the head of Miles Canyon, to be carried on flatcars pulled by horses or mules around the canyon and the two sets of rapids below the canyon. The rails of the crude tramway were made of logs.

bloodthirsty brutes defied us to sleep. Not for an instant did they stop their ceaseless hum-m-m-m. They were particulary "hellish" in this district, especially if we camped on the low-lying places. We soon learned to choose our camp sites on high banks where, if a stiff breeze were blowing, we were not troubled.

After we got through the Five Fingers, so named because of five huge rocks rising like sentries in midstream of the upper Yukon River, the navigation was fairly smooth. Day after day we passed unbroken mountain ranges and wooded river banks—a sameness of scenery which became monotonous.

Every day we travelled eight hours, sailing when the wind was up, rowing or floating with the current when the wind was down. Every evening we made camp, rolling in our blankets on piles of pine boughs in the open, or sleeping under canvas if it were raining.

We cooked our meals on a little sheet-iron Klondyke stove, and there was generally an unlimited supply of dry wood for the gathering. At first we had no big game, but our men shot a few squirrels, which for a time I could not eat until driven to it by a craving for fresh meat. Occasionally we had a wild fowl, and, as we neared Dawson, we were able to buy pieces of moose or caribou from the Indians.

All along the way we fished—trolling for trout from the boat. I caught a salmon trout weighing 9 pounds, but others weighed over 12 pounds. George speared many whitefish or cast for grayling in some quiet pool of water.

We picked wild berries of all kinds—raspberries, strawberries, red currants, blueberries, and cranberries, but we sorely missed fresh vegetables. On a solitary berry-picking excursion I came upon a party of Indians in a fine swampy patch of blueberries. They took no notice of me, and I stayed so long picking and having my fill that George was worried and came looking for me. He always wanted me to take a revolver when I went away from camp, but I had no fear of anything, expecially if I had a stout stick.

As over the Pass, we continued to be part of a never-ending procession. Boats of all kinds passed us—singly, in pairs, in fleets: scows, canoes, small sailboats, rafts, and row boats—anything that would float. One boat was actually cut in half—evidently the last word in a 50-50 division of an outfit—so many partners were quarrelling and quitting. How most of these boats, with pilots knowing little of swift-water navigation, got through the canyon, rapids, and Five Fingers, was little short of miraculous.

In camps we met hundreds of men of all sorts, and without exception, they were kindly and courteous. One party included an undertaker, doctor, druggist, and nurse, to whom I suggested that they fly a black flag with skull and crossbones. This was the beginning of some fine friendships which have lasted to this day.

Two nights above Dawson we made an afternoon camp on a creek tributary to the Yukon, where a few miners had struck it. At first we were greeted coldly, as there is nothing more dreaded by real miners than a stampede. Besides, it was a late discovery, none of the claims had been recorded, and it was a rare opportunity for claim-jumping.

As the day went on our neighbours became more friendly. All were from New Zealand, and they thought of naming the creek "Maori." I chose Excelsior, which they liked, and so it is named to this day. I invited them to supper, which was extra special, being hard tack, coffee and dried apple dumpling. The New Zealanders said it was their first dinner party in the Canadian North, and the best meal they had had since leaving home.

Next morning George and I staked claims and proceeded on the last lap of this long journey.   ⇒⋙⋘

Chapter VI
DAWSON CITY IN '98-'99

It took us 12 days to make the trip from Lake Bennett to Dawson that summer of '98. As we neared our journey's end the scenery became less rugged, the mountains changed to high hills, the Yukon flowed more placidly. At last, rounding a bend during the afternoon of 5th August, we came within sight of the city, "the end of the rainbow where we would find our pot of gold." In the distance the many columns of smoke, rising from the buildings, were a welcome sign of settlement and civilization to our eyes so long accustomed to the vast uninhabited hinterland.

We skirted the small wooded islands above the mouth of the Klondyke River which empties into the Yukon, and there, scattered on the flats at the junction of the rivers, and straggling half-way to the top of the high hill behind "King Solomon's Dome," lay Dawson, a city of tents, shanties, and log cabins, with a floating population of approximately 20,000. On landing, even in our most enthusiastic moments, we could not have said the place was beautiful. It was like every new town in the making, disordered and untidy. On the waterfront were hundreds of boats tied to wharves or beached on the muddy shore. Everywhere were rough board buildings on stilts; hurriedly pitched tents, with stoves, cooking utensils, and bundles thrown around; and freshly cleared lots, with new one-room shacks, bushes, and shavings strewn about.

The only semblance of order was on Front Street, which probably was due to the fact that the Mounted Police had put up notices that all lumber, logs, timber, cordwood, and other obstructions be removed; that campers occupying the streets must move their tents elsewhere because the health of the town was threatened (there were already many cases of malaria, typhoid fever, and a few of smallpox). The street was flanked with two-storey log or frame buildings, very large tents, through which streamed the stampeders, now in a frenzied hurry to stake their claims. Almost every other building was either a dance hall, saloon, hotel, or restaurant, with such names as Floradora, Aurora, Northern, Monte Carlo, M. and N. (the name derived from the initials of the owners' names), Sourdough, Can Can, and Chisholm's Saloon, nicknamed the "Bucket of Blood," where the first drink was accompanied by a whisk. (What for? To brush you off when you came to.) One or the other told the world by painted signs and printed notices that "crap, chuck, and draw poker, blackjack, roulette wheels, and faro banks were run by the management; that every known fluid—water excepted—was for sale at the bar; that there were special rates for the 'gambling perfesh.'"

Front Street was the first in Dawson City to develop a businesslike look. The tents and shanties of the first arrivals were replaced by log or frame buildings—many carrying rather elaborate and pretentious signs.

Our first business was to get a home. Looking about Dawson we found lot prices sky-high, and lumber selling at $100 to $500 per thousand. Hearing that there was plenty of land for the taking on the other side of the Klondyke, we decided to go there. We squatted on the hill above Lousetown, described by the sourdoughs as "The lousiest place on God's earth, for any day the lice might walk away with them buildin's," a mile and a half from Dawson, our men building the largest of a hundred or so cabins.

It contained one large room, a small corner "stateroom" for me, and the usual built-in bunks for the men. Instead of the dirt floor, we pounded into the earth small round poplar blocks, which not only made the place warmer, but was a convenience in cleaning, as I swept the dirt into the numerous cracks. The men made our furniture from tree-trunks and twigs, boards, and packing-cases. It included plain willow-withy chairs, with an armchair for me, a board bench, a table (two wide boards nailed to four slim poplar legs), and a packing-box cupboard and dressing-table.

I have always liked fixing up homes, and although this was only a little northern cabin I tried to make it as pretty and homey as possible. Much against the will of the party I had brought two linen tablecloths with two dozen napkins, silver knives, forks, and spoons for company, and a bolt of cretonne—a gay pattern of Marechal Neil roses on a sage-green background. I made this into curtains, packing-box covers, and, later, cushions which I filled with feathers of wild ducks. It was well worth the trouble of bringing as it did brighten the little cabin. I pinned our surplus blankets on the walls, put our fur robes on the bunks, laid the table with coloured oilcloth which I scalloped with scissors, placed on it a bouquet of wild flowers in a tin can covered with birchbark, and arrayed my agate iron dishes and silver in the cupboard. When we were completely settled we were all proud of our little home.

And now to claim my treasure—the million dollars of gold dust—while the menfolk staked and worked their claims. One day George remonstrated with me on the use of some strong words of the North which I was rapidly adopting. "Polly, what will people think of you if you talk like that when we get home?"

"Think of me! If I get my half-million I won't give a damn; and if I don't, then they won't give a damn for me!"

My first visit was made to the Gold Commissioner's office, where, with blissful ignorance, I laid my case before various officials, asking to be shown the records. After considerable palm-crossing these were produced. There was much crooked work done by government officials in those days. Changes were made in records by running a pen through names and dates, by erasing or scratching out names, and, in some instances, names, date, and all information were cut out entirely and a fresh slip pasted in.

At the post office I asked for information about the men whose names were signed as witnesses to the Lambert will. I was told that mail was being held there for them, and so I wrote to them. Receiving no replies, I wrote other letters and registered them. Some of these were delivered but never answered.

Finally, on payment of $100, a post office employee (now deceased) opened the letters of these witnesses and gave them to me to read. I had hoped to get much information, but did not get any. The post office employee returned the letters to their envelopes and wrote across them "opened by mistake."

So I went on and on, tipping and tipping until money was getting perilously low. Summer ended and still I hoped and sought vainly for the Lambert grave, the witnesses of the will, the registration of the claims, and the gold dust. After exhausting every clue I gave up, convinced the whole affair was either a huge hoax or an unfathomable mystery. All I discovered was that Lambert actually had existed; that he had been a prospector in the far corners of the North for many years; that he had last been heard of in Juneau, Alaska; that the will was in his handwriting; and then information petered out.

Later I learned that the Lamberts, losing faith in me because of my failure to return within six months with the gold dust, interested a man by the name of Gillette (the Chicago yeast and baking-powder man). He put up several thousand dollars for one of the Lamberts who, accompanied by a lawyer, started for Dawson. After hearing the horrible tales, and fearful of attempting the Pass, they decided to enter the country by St. Michaels. They reached that port, and I was told that the young attorney, who had been particularly loud in his expressions of what he was going to do to me when they caught me with the stolen million, was separated from Lambert, his purpose, and pocketbook by one of the peroxide beauties of the North, who found many an Eldorado in such simple-minded men. However, I did get the proverbial comfort of misery, for at least I had company. Their search came to nothing, even as did mine, and the Lambert case forever will remain one of the unsolved mysteries of the North.

The glorious days of the northern Indian summer came. The *Klondyke Nugget*, the first newspaper in Dawson, was warning chechakos unprepared for an Arctic winter to leave the country at once; that winter set in in September; that floating ice from the upper rivers made navigation on the Yukon dangerous until early November; that severe storms and cold were to be expected at this time; that to spend a winter in a tent was risking one's life; that the rubber footwear brought by most of us was useless for the northern winter. Everyone who could was hurrying out as fast as possible. A Mountie told me that there remained less than 15,000 of the 40,000 who had stampeded in, and before spring another 5,000 would be gone.

The "Sand Bar" in front of the city had been laid out in two streets, both lined with outfits for sale. Some were auctioned at ridiculously low prices, and even at that there were few buyers.

As I watched the ever-departing stream I thought how only a few short months ago we, who had staked all and strained every muscle to get into the country, were now making every sacrifice to get out. I, too, must leave.

I had given myself so completely to the search for the Lambert gold that I had deliberately put out of mind a terrible suspicion—I was to become a mother. I could not believe it. I would not let my mind dwell on it. I pursued my quest with feverish energy. My suspicion became a certainty. Terror-stricken, I faced this Gethsemane. I realized I could not leave the country. I could never walk back over that Pass. Neither could I face the ravaging ordeal before me alone, helpless, most of my money gone. Life had trapped me. "Oh God, my Father, let this cup pass from me," I prayed. "Let me die."

Today I am glad that my Maker did not answer my prayer. Here I would like to tell young mothers who face this bearing of unwanted babies in dire circumstances, who rebel against it with every fibre of their being, to keep their faith in God. This trust saw me through. I was brought up in the belief that no one is called upon to bear a greater burden than he can carry. I often thought of the guiding principle of Mother's life, "The Lord will provide."

I told my brother.

"I never should have consented to your coming," he said.

"Father will never forgive me." His helplessness to cope with the situation bucked me up. He told our cousin, Harry Peachey, who was planning to leave the country. Afterwards, Aunt Martha Morse told me that when he arrived home he said, "By this time Martha is dead. She was going to have a baby, and she couldn't possibly live, she looked so ill."

My old fighting spirit came to the rescue. I determined I would not brood over my troubles. I would not be downed. I suppose it is the pioneer spirit, not to be overwhelmed by trouble, but to arise and go forth to meet it. Besides, I had the little one to think of now. I must make some clothes. I looked over our outfit. There were the tablecloths and the two dozen table-napkins (and didn't they come in handy!). As I sewed on the little garments, I became fully resigned to the baby's coming. I began to have a real joy in its anticipation. I knew that if I got through safely and my baby was well, I would have many happy hours caring for him, and when the Yukon River broke up in the spring we would go out to our dear ones.

And, just as the summer days were light so long, now the winter days grew darker and darker, until it was continuous night. Endless days with no sight of sun. Deep blue nights with countless stars paling in the Milky Way. Cold, still, aurora nights, with red, gold, and green northern lights, crackling and swishing as they streamed from the dusky skyline to the very zenith of the heavens. Pale, green, moonlight nights, the Great Dipper, and, almost above us, the Pole Star, fixed, constant, comforting.

After the supper dishes were done, if I sewed, as a special favour I was allowed two candles. None of us liked cards, but we spent many evenings playing checkers and chess on home-made boards. Sometimes I wrote or read, or became interested in the nautical problems worked out by our two sea captains. Yet, in spite of high resolves, there were many nights of heartache and homesickness. If we sang, which was rarely, "Home Sweet Home" was never allowed. One night I took down the photographs of my parents and children; they aggravated my loneliness.

We had many regrets for our high living of the early winter months. We did not realize the problem of a food shortage and the terrific winter prices which were to add to my troubles of that lonely winter. It became necessary to ration ourselves, and I determined that I would share as the men. For six months we were to be entirely without butter, sugar, or milk. Our breakfast consisted of corn meal mush with molasses and clear coffee. Flour was $1 a pound, meat $2 a pound, butter $3 a pound, eggs $3 a dozen, oranges, apples, and onions $1.50 each—when they could be had. Cow's milk was $16 a gallon, but hay was $400 a ton. How I longed for a change of diet—some fruit and vegetables! Instead I gulped down the ever-unpalatable corn meal mush, prunes, and tea with no milk or sugar.

Word spread about the camp that a baby was expected. I had not found a million dollars in gold dust—but I made a rich discovery. Always, the world over, pioneers have proven themselves to be salt of the earth. They have a fine courage, which they know how to keep alive in each. They know how to share their few possessions. The gifts those men brought me! One stampeder's wife had insisted that he bring a bolt of red flannel for abdominal bands, and over he came with yards of it. Others brought me cherished pots of home-made jam—another, a tablecloth for baby dresses, and delicacies for my Christmas dinner. Showered with kindnesses like these, I learned to love my fellow men of the North, who, although I did not know it at the time, were to be my people for the rest of my life.

There was also the immediate problem of financing my confinement. I went to see Father Judge (head of the Roman Catholic mission and hospital). He told me my hospital and doctor's expenses would be $1,000. He was kind, and offered to trust me until I could get money in the spring. I was brought up to abhor debt. I had had two children, and had the advantage of the most expert medical care in Chicago. I decided to get through alone.

The baby came ahead of time. I was alone, and it was over quickly, an incredibly easy birth—Mother Nature's gift to women who live a natural out-of-door life such as I had done. And weren't the menfolk surprised, when they returned from work at night, to find, wrapped in red flannel—a fine, healthy boy! My brother nearly passed out when he had to give him his first bath. They called him the little chechako, but I immediately named him Lyman after Grandfather Munger.

I had not written of my condition to my parents. I reasoned that they could do nothing, and it would mean weeks of worry. Now that the baby was here, I could hardly wait until my hand grew steady enough to write them this news.

"February 10, 1899.

"On Tuesday, at noon, January 31st, my third son was born, and I welcomed him with delight. He weighs nine pounds, and is as hale and hearty as any baby born under happier conditions. I have written this little poem about him:

THE LITTLE CHECHAKO

His eyes are bright as midnight stars,
His hair it shines like gold of Mars,
He bears no pack, he wears no clothes,
From tip of head to tip of toes
His body's red, just like a rose.

"I am enclosing a curl of his hair. Embrace my other little ones for me. Tell them about their new little brother, and be ready to welcome the wanderers."

Being young, and, now I realize, blessed with an unusually good constitution, I was soon up and around.

What a welcome the camp gave my baby! The men of our party, and my neighbours, all men, took full charge. They kept the fires going. They brought in foodstuffs—fresh-baked bread, cakes, chocolates, ptarmigan, moosemeat, every wild delicacy of the country. Miners, prospectors, strange uncouth men called to pay their respects. They brought gifts of olive oil (which by some miraculous mistake had been shipped in with foodstuffs), gold nuggets, gold dust. Often as I lay in bed with the baby I thought of the Holy Mother and her Babe, born in a manger, and the gifts of frankincense and myrrh brought to her by the wise men.

With tears in their eyes my visitors told me of their own babies so far away. They wanted to hold mine, to see his toes, to feel his tiny fingers curl in their rough hands, to see for themselves that his back was straight and strong. Later, his bath hour became a daily show. Again the dishpan was pressed into service, and what nobler use for a dishpan? The cabin, which was stifling hot for fear the baby would catch cold, became hotter and more stifling. My heart was touched and responded to this adoration, for every mother knows that there is only one perfect baby in the world and that one

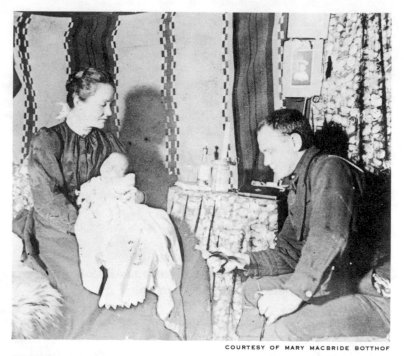

Martha Louise, her new son Lyman, and her brother George in the tiny Dawson City cabin. On the wall are photos of her two older boys, Donald and Warren.

is her own. From the moment of his arrival little Lyman was the happiest, most contented child I ever knew. He would go to the roughest-looking of them all, gurgling and laughing and pulling their beards.

Our cabin became a social centre. Again we brought out the mandolin and guitar, and the stillness of the North was broken with such rollicking songs as "Johnny Schmoker, Johnny Schmoker," "There is a Tavern in the Town," and the ever popular "Bicycle Built for Two." Then our spirits would effervesce and we would sing that greatest home song ever written—"Swanee River," our eyes growing misty at the words:

> *All de world am sad and dreary,*
> *Everywhere I roam,*
> *Oh! Darkies, how my heart grows weary*
> *Far from de old folks at home.*

Chapter VII
A WILD WINTER IN DAWSON

So popular did our home musicales become that we were offered what we thought was a fabulously large sum to "put on a turn" at the Pavilion—a variety theatre, the first of its kind in Yukon. It had been opened in the summer of '98 shortly before our arrival. Its advent was contemporaneous with the coming of the Salvation Army, the organization of the first masonic lodge, the establishment of the "elegant parlours" of the first professional masseuse, who advertised "Russian, Turkish, plain, and medicated baths." The Pavilion was very popular, one of its chief attractions being the beautiful and vivacious Oatley Sisters, who had good voices and good figures, sang the latest songs, and danced the buck and wing with abandon. Although I needed the money I never could quite bring myself to consider going on its programme.

It was a wild winter in Dawson that winter of '98. As I look back to it I have an infinite pity for the men of those days, many of superior breeding and education. They were lonely, disillusioned, and discouraged. There were so few places to go where it was bright and cheerful. They gathered with the others in the saloons and dance halls. They joined the party with the first round, and then they drank to drown their woes. The continued Arctic darkness contributed to the debauchery. Revellers lost all sense of time as to day and night periods, and attuned themselves to the ever-present night until they passed out from sheer exhaustion.

Analysing the women of the Klondyke stampede, there were three classes: members of the oldest profession in the world, who ever follow armies and gold rushes; dance hall and variety girls, whose business was to entertain and be dancing partners; and a few others, wives with unbounded faith in and love for their mates, or the odd person like myself on a special mission.

While I did not enter into the gaiety, I did have what sporting editors would call a ringside seat. We did not know when we squatted above Lousetown that we had established ourselves just above the red-light district, through which we had to pass to reach the footbridge across the Klondyke River to Dawson. As I walked back and forth I often saw the painted women, leaning over their half-doors, brazenly soliciting trade. Clearly through the still, cold night air would come the sounds of wild revelry . . . the tinny piano pounded by the "professor" . . . loud laughter . . . singing.

While many prostitutes, in their isolated cabins, practised their profession quite independently, there were also some white slave girls, mostly Belgians. These had been brought in and were managed by men known as *macques*, who not only lived "off the avails," but first demanded repayment of the passage money of their victims. Let it be always be the credit of the North West Mounted Police that they spared no efforts to bring these men of fancy dress and patent leather shoes to justice. They were ruthlessly rounded up, brought to trial, and, if proven guilty, given a blue ticket, which meant shoved aboard a boat and told to "get to hell out of the country and never come back."

The dance hall girls were often beautiful, invariably had good figures, and many were clever and resented the stigma generally attached to their profession. They had to be able to do some vaudeville stunt, and to be entertaining companions—the kind "a fella would like to buy a drink for." It was decidedly to their personal advantage to have a flair for salesmanship, to help the proprietor sell his full stock of liquor, for they received a commission of 25 or 50 per cent on drinks, which were never less than $1 apiece. It was said that some girls made as high as $250 a night, but this could only be done by "rolling," which meant getting a man drunk and stealing his poke.

The dance-saloon-gambling-variety halls were built on the same order, the bars usually to the left of the entrance. They were backed with plate glass mirrors on the upper wall, and the lower was lined with bottle-laden shelves. On the hardwood counters rested several finely balanced gold scales for weighing dust, as there was practically no currency in the country. (An ounce of dust was worth $15.)

To the right were the gambling rooms, usually furnished with poker and crap tables and chairs, faro banks, and roulette wheels. Although there was generally a house limit on the bets, sometimes the games were wide open, as high as $20,000 being lost in a single whirl of the roulette wheel, $5,000 at stud poker, and $1,000 a throw in a crap game. (Speaking of bets, I knew two old sourdoughs who bet each other $10,000 on their respective spitting accuracy—the mark being a crack in the wall.)

Dance and variety halls had fine floors and were lighted by hanging oil lamps. There was always good music, some of the musicians having played in the best orchestras in America. The larger halls had stages and galleries, with curtained boxes, where patrons might have a certain privacy for entertaining their girl friends or watching shows and dances. Drinks served here cost double.

Dances were $1 apiece, and each was concluded with a "promenade all" to the bar, where the male dancer would buy two drinks, ginger ale for his girl partner, and generally hard liquor for himself. If he fancied champagne, he paid $30 a pint.

A woman whose husband was accidentally killed on the Pass was forced to earn a living for their child, who was at home with relatives. She had a very sweet voice, which one of the dance hall owners had heard on the boat trip in, when she sang a number of old-fashioned songs. He learned of her trouble, and, realizing that her voice would be a "gold mine" for his dance hall, offered her a good salary to sing each night. She consented on the understanding that she would do only her turn and go.

She told me of the sickening dread of her first appearance. On entering she was confronted by a palatial bar, which was lined with drinkers; and bartenders were "setting 'em up" as fast as possible. A great crowd was dancing wildly, reeling madly. The noise was frightening—piano banging, glasses clinking, hysterical laughter mingled with oaths, talking, shouting—Dog-faced Kitty trying to teach a sourdough to waltz, and Sunshine Sue in the arms of "her man."

My friend had chosen for her opening number, "Don't you remember sweet Alice, Ben Bolt?" As the first notes floated through that place of drunken revelry a hush fell upon the crowd, broken only by a high, shrill voice, "Look who's here!" and followed by, "You shut yer trap!"

When she finished the men surged round her, but the proprietor was as good as his word. "No, boys, Mrs. S———— will sing here every night if she's left alone. Her husband was killed on the Pass. She has a child to support. Will you play the game?" A roar of "Yes!" filled the hall.

Strange women drifted into the Klondyke, their very names descriptive of some characteristic—names that now are a part of Yukon history—and, with no intention of casting slurs upon any, let me tell you some. There was Diamond-Tooth Gertie, a pretty, dark young woman who had a diamond inset in one of her front teeth; Sweet Marie, who nearly killed a man who put her beloved "Fido" under a tub and piled it high with furniture and bedding; Spanish Jeanette, who, when she said she was a lady from Castile, provoked this now historic remark from a sourdough, "Castile? Hell! You sure don't get to the castile (soap) often enough. A Mexican from Market Street, 'Frisco, more likely!"

I remember hearing of Lime Juice Lil, who, as her name suggests, was a teetotaller. She was notorious for "rolling," and finally the police got the goods on her and she received a summons, which she knew meant the blue ticket. She secured an interview with the Commissioner. Quietly dressed in a tailored suit, accompanied by a woman in widow's weeds, she arrived. The widow told how this *good* woman had helped her starving children—that they would have died if it had not been for this *good* woman. Then Lime Juice Lil spoke up. She was in love with one of the bartenders of the town. In fact, they were planning to get married. With muffled sobs she confessed that it was very necessary that they get married, for she was going to have a baby. The sympathetic Commissioner (not at all taken in) voiced the opinion that matters would be simplified greatly if the marriage took place at once. It did, but no child ever blessed the union.

Many of these girls had hearts of gold. They would give their last dollar to those who needed it. I have wondered since if we other women could not have been kinder to those so set apart from us. Too often many of us, secure in our legitimacy, swanked by arrogantly. I was told that the girls often laughed over this among themselves, for well they knew the double life of many of the leading citizens.

Most of the girls paid the price of this gay wild life in full. The longest they could stand its fast pace was five to ten years. Is it any wonder that they "cashed in," for they were well aware if they saved no stake they would die in the gutter.

Likewise numbers of men burned themselves out by their hard living in these early Klondyke days. I have known many who died from drink and dissipation in the prime of their lives.

As I was busy with the baby, the days now passed more quickly. There were times when I missed and longed for the comforts of civilization, but when I heard of the death of a young mother leaving a baby girl 10 days old, I realized I was fortunate. I was glad, too, that we had not built our cabin in Dawson City, where typhoid and malaria raged that winter.

In April many men who had been laid up all winter became excitingly busy working their claims. They cleared away the snow in the shafts, built huge fires, shovelled and picked the thawed ground, and then rebuilt the fires. This was the last year of this old-fashioned and slow type of placer mining, for steam thawing machines were shipped in on the railway next year, and high prices were paid for contracts—the faster the work the higher the price.

The hills purpled with spring flowers—the dainty pasque flower or crocus, protected from the frosts of night with a soft downy collar. I watched the purple petals fall, the seeds form into lovely plumrose tufts, and the remarkable growth of foliage. Altogether I found 11 varieties of this ranunculaceae family, including the tiny yellow water crowfoot, commonly skirting the edges of sluggish streams and sloughs, and the long-fruited anemone, with its pretty white blossoms shading into delicate greens and blues.

I continued to have many visitors to see the baby. One day a man from Chicago called. In the conversation, when he mentioned such

Martha Louise's first Yukon home was above Lousetown, in the shadow of the hill behind Klondyke city. They crossed the river to Dawson by footbridge.

names as Charles Morse, I naturally said, "He's an uncle of mine," or Lyman J. Gage, "I've known him for years." Next day a Mountie dropped in, and we chatted informally. Later I learned that he had come at the instigation of my Chicago visitor, who had reported to the police that there was a crazy woman with a baby "all alone in a cabin on the hill," who said she was related to, and knew, some of the big men in Chicago; that if this were true, she wouldn't be stranded up there; and the matter should be investigated.

One spring evening, April 26, 1899, I was looking toward Dawson, and saw many tongues of fire darting through clouds of smoke. It was the big fire that burned half the city. Like the Chicago fire, it was alleged, but never proven, to have been started by the upsetting of a lamp. There was a southwest wind blowing; the firemen lost considerable time in getting the new fire apparatus (shipped in after the fall fire) into working order, and in the meantime the fire leaped from building to building, the rough boards, oakum and moss-chinked logs, canvas roofs and factory cotton linings, burning like paper. The loss was estimated at half a million dollars, yet before the ashes were cold they were being panned for gold, and rebuilding had started.

Then came that time in the North, "when the days begin to lengthen and the sun begins to strengthen," when all eyes are constantly watching the streams and lakes of the Yukon River system for signs of the annual break-up. It is then that chechakos become sourdoughs. Now my time had come, for had I not watched the river freeze in the fall, and was I not about to see the majestic Yukon begin again its northern rush to the Arctic?

Well do I remember that momentous date, May 23, 1899—the day I became a sourdough. I was sitting in front of my cabin, little Lyman asleep in a swing made from a packing-box. Above was a perfect blue sky, the sun shining with such brilliance that the glare dazzled my eyes as I looked into the distance. Below, the Yukon was heaving, cracking, and groaning, for the ice and snow were melting fast. A warm, gentle breeze was scattering the yellow pollen of the willow buds.

Suddenly, hearing an unusual rustling, I looked up and saw a movement in the bushes on the hillside above me. Thinking it was a bear, I hastily snatched Lyman and rushed into the cabin. I made him comfortable on my bunk, put up the shutters on the one small window, gathered up all the firearms—two revolvers, two shotguns, a rifle, and the ammunition, and took them outside. With nervous fingers I loaded them.

I was still on the lookout for my first bear, and was thinking what glory would be mine if I should kill one while alone in camp. I'd show the men of our party that I could use a gun as well as any of them. What if she had cubs? Absorbed in these thoughts, still conscious of the rustling, grinding noises, I had not looked toward the hill. When I did, to my horror I saw the whole hillside slowly moving toward the cabin, and gaining momentum. A landslide! The quick thaw had loosened the upper stratum of earth and made it into a river of mud that was carrying everything before it.

I dashed into the cabin again. I seized the baby, wrapped him in a shawl, put on my own coat, and paralysed with fright, stood at the corner of the cabin, wondering desperately what move to make, if any. I knew I was in terrible danger, and in silent prayer I commended myself and baby to the care of my Maker.

God answered my prayer. The onrushing avalanche was halted by a clump of trees 70 feet above the cabin. The mud, rocks, snow, and small trees piled up against them. Deeply rooted, they held firmly. In a moment the roaring river of mud started to move again, but the trees had split the avalanche. The heavier right half cleared our cabin, uprooted a tree, and swept with it two cabins below, depositing its debris on the bosom of the Yukon. The left passed more closely, carried with it our outhouses, and finally lost itself in the more securely frozen ground below us.

Realizing our narrow escape from a horrible death, and trembling from head to foot, I tottered into the cabin. I must have fainted, for when I came to, several hours later, I was lying on my bunk with my little one beside me. We were both unharmed. Subconsciously I must have taken care not to fall upon him. Looking out, I knew that it was not a bad dream, for the hillside was cleared of its surface, and gleamed like the earth of a new-cut furrow.

Hearing the terrific barking of dogs, I went to the door. I gazed upon a scene of magnificent beauty—enormous ice-blocks coursing down the river, swirling in swift-frothing eddies. And, sitting on a huge ice-cake, hurtling by in mid-stream, was a bobcat, with a frantic pack of huskies in hot pursuit along the river bank. As though the poor beast had not trouble enough! The river was clearing fast.

I had become a sourdough.

Chapter VIII
I GO OUT

Every day, that spring of '99, numbers of steamers, barges, scows, canoes, and rafts plied up and down the river. Thirty sacks of mail came in on the *Flora*, and among my letters I received one mailed in Chicago the previous August. There was no letter from Will. Evidently he had taken me at my word. More than ever I was determined never to go back to him. The river craft brought in shipments of food, and I was thankful for the change and the summer prices. Fresh milk was now only $1 a quart—one-fourth the winter price. There was an abundance of fresh fish—salmon being only 20 cents a pound. Eggs, sugar, oranges, lemons, and vegetables were still unobtainable. I could now get a bottle of Castoria for the baby for $1.50; in the winter I had paid the hospital $2 for a partly filled bottle—the only one in the whole camp.

May merged into June—the loveliest month of all the year in this land of the midnight sun. The trees budded into leaf and the ground and hillsides were carpeted with wild flowers—the dainty pyrola, or "shin plant"; the wild Arctic poppy; the showy bluebell, mistakenly called Virginia cowslip; Jacob's ladder, unkindly named "skunkweed," because of its disagreeable odour; the calypso, said to have originated from the ground watered by the tears shed by the goddess Calypso over the desertion of Odysseus, who was wrecked on her Isles, and to whom she promised immortality if he would marry her; the delicate coral root and the lady's tresses—all to be found within a few minutes' walk of my cabin.

The men would mind the baby in the evening as I roamed the sandy, sunny hills, or the low boggy places on an orchid hunt. I found many varieties, the most common being the white orchis, with large purply-pink blotches, usually one flower on an erect stem, with two or three sheath-like leaves. I discovered the Siberian orchis, or Franklin lady slipper (so called because it was first mentioned by the botanist of the Franklin expedition), its pure white sack with purple spots inside, and green overhanging lip, matching its two wings.

Again I write home—July 4, 1899:

"It is a gala day in Dawson, and the Canadians are seemingly delighted to help us celebrate our national holiday as we were to join with them on Dominion Day (July 1). In fact, the celebration has been a continued spree, the all-time daylight making many think there is no bedtime.

"The Fourth was heralded in by a gunshot, one minute after midnight, and 10,000 Americans and Canadians paraded up and down singing alternately 'My Country 'tis of Thee,' and 'God Save the Queen.' The terrific uproar of unusual noises frightened hundreds of dogs that had never before heard such a racket, and they rushed madly up and down the streets or jumped into the river, to swim across to more silent places.

"What's a Fourth without fireworks? We had them too, but the beautiful colour effect was lost entirely in the daylight.

"In the afternoon there was a baseball game on the Sand Bar between the 'Sourdough Stiffs' and the 'Chechakos,' the bats made of boat masts and the balls of twine or wood blocks.

"The thermometer registered 98 above in the middle of the day, but, as usual, the night is getting cool.

"A brickyard four or five miles above us on Swede Creek is working full blast now, and a bricklayer told me he had a contract for putting up one of the first brick buildings in Dawson at $30 a day.

"Hundreds of people are leaving the country daily, but this creates a greater opportunity for those who remain. We hear rumours of a stampede to Cape Nome on American territory.

"Those who remain are very much for, or very much against, the country. There is no half-way feeling. Yet as a new country it does not present the serious problems that confronted the little band of Pilgrim Fathers who landed at Plymouth Rock. Health, determination, and self-denial are necessary for success here.

"I miss my little ones, but I am planning many things for them.

"The banks of the Yukon are now becoming vividly spotted with a variety of vetches, the golden rod, and the wonderfully brilliant magenta vines."

One day toward the end of July Father unexpectedly walked in. My joy was unbounded, and his was too, especially when I showed him my beautiful baby son, who held out his arms to him.

"Daughter, I have come to take you back," he said, and added quickly, "Have you heard from Will?"

"I have not. Nor do I want to hear from him—nor see him again," I reiterated emphatically.

"I cannot understand any man allowing his wife to go alone on such a trip as this—not even accepting his legal responsibility," commented Father. "I want to take you away from all this hardship."

Suddenly his eyes rested on the wall behind the stove. A horrified look came into them as he pointed to many skin-covered cartons on a shelf there and shouted to my brother:

"George, are you crazy? Dynamite over a stove!"

We soon assured him that the dangerous-looking packages contained nothing more deadly than our desiccated vegetables and powdered soups. We had grown to hate their taste too; "desecrated" we called them now.

We decided to celebrate Father's coming by a good meal. A scow of foodstuffs had come in that very day. My brother George was elected to do the marketing, and he returned with a half-pound of moose liver, to be fried with bacon, one medium-sized onion, and one huge potato, these vegetables costing $1 apiece. No more could be purchased, and one of each to a family was considered a fair allotment to the many eager buyers.

The cooking of the vegetables was a matter of grave discussion. It was agreed finally to fry the onion and bake the potato, because the latter could then be eaten skin and all. I had a few bad moments when the thought occurred to me—what if the potato has a bad heart! Large potatoes sometimes have. But it hadn't, and never was a meal enjoyed more thoroughly—even our dessert, which was brown bread without butter, tea without sugar, rice, and molasses.

Father was eager for me to leave as soon as possible, "Catalpa Knob is a wonderful place," he said, "healthy for the elder boys, perfect for the baby, much better than this crude cabin. And now that you are determined you will never go back to Will, there's not a reason in the world why you should not come to live in your Father's home again."

Then I told him of the new life I intended to make for myself in this new country—of the placer claims I'd staked on Excelsior Creek. We finally agreed that we would leave these in my brother George's care, and if they did not yield at least $10,000 before the next year I would never mention "Klondyke" again.

We booked our passage on the *Canadian*, which, like the *Utopia* which brought us in, was crowded to the "gunnels" with people, baggage, and boxes of gold dust worth hundreds of thousands of dollars. We had an uneventful journey until we came to Five Fingers. Going downstream was easy compared to upstream. Now the swift, seething waters, forced between the narrow rocks, piled high, and our steamer had to mount her way. As she entered one of the whirlpools she lurched toward one Finger and smashed part of her upper deck to kindling. For a second her wreck seemed inevitable, but skillful navigating saved her. Once again, breathing freely, we were on our way.

At Whitehorse we left the steamer and went round the portage in a tram. Being on the outskirts of settlement we were accompanied by an armed escort of Mounted Police, because of our gold dust. I never knew of any gold-stealing holdups on the hinterland trails or waterways in the early days. This was due probably to the impossibility of getting the "loot" out of the country by the main routes, and any attempt to blaze a new trail, especially in winter, invariably meant death. Besides, those were the days when the Mounted Police were building up that world-famed reputation— "They always get their man."

At the end of the portage we boarded a small river steamer and had a pleasant trip through the lakes to Bennett, where we took the train over the new narrow-gauge railway to Skagway.

This road was just completed, and literally had been blasted out of the face of the rocky wall of the gorge, on which it gradually wound down to the stony bottoms of the Skagway River.

As we went over the Pass in the train we caught glimpses of the old trail. I recalled vividly the agony of the year before. Once again in my memory I staggered up and up. Dead Horse Gulch brought back to me the screams of dying horses.

It took only two hours to make that downward trip from the summit to the town—in complete comfort and enjoyment, over a road on which, only a year ago, thousands had sweated blood for two days.

Skagway, too, had changed. The wild lawless town had become a well-ordered place of 10,000 people, with several first-class hotels and a daily newspaper.

The homeward trip was wonderful—Lyman was, as usual, good, and a general favourite with everybody. Father and I contributed songs and riddles to the programmes which are always part of ship life. And what do you suppose I ordered for my first outside meal? Tenderloin steak, a double order of French fried potatoes, olives, and ice cream!

We arrived at Catalpa Knob safely. I have no adequate words to describe that home-coming—reunited with my little ones and my dear parents! The ranch was a gorgeous spectacle of beauty and plenty. The ranch house seemed huge in contrast to my Klondyke cabin home. Father, always a good provider, had grown an abundance on his fertile acres—an abundance not only for his family and friends but even for wayfarers. How different from the North, I thought, where I had to count so carefully each potato, onion, egg, or orange, where the struggle for existence had been such a battle, where Nature's first law—the survival of the fittest—had demanded such a gruelling day-by-day observance.

Father and Mother were so kind to me. As always, they seemed to understand. There was no trace of long-suffering duty in this consideration. Time and time again Mother said, "Daughter, it is good to have you and your children in your father's house again. I love to hear the children's voices as they laugh and play." And they adored the baby.

In such a setting I suppose I should have been content—yet I wasn't. For a time I rested in the peace, plenty, and security of it. Then came the dark short days of November, when the Kansas winter sets in. Days and days of mournful winds and cyclonic dust storms, which later turned into howling, blinding blizzards. The snow whirled and drifted. When the helpers left for the barns they had to tie long ropes as guide lines to the doors to enable them to find their way back.

Shut in for days, time began to hang heavily. There were too many long hours—with nothing to do. I brooded upon my troubles. My marriage had been a failure. My Klondyke trip had been a failure. Even my children seemingly had no urgent need of me. Father and Mother surrounded them with every care and kindness. I was only 33 years old. So many years stretched ahead of me—interminable—uninteresting. Somehow the mainspring of my life had snapped, my zest for life, for adventure was no more. I lost interest in my clothes—which to a woman of my temperament who loves pretty things is one of the last props. I pulled my hair back from my face and wound it in a tight little knob at the back of my head. My weight went down to 90 pounds. Silently, moodily, I went around—not even rising to the emotional relief of tears.

Gradually, I began to get a new perspective of life—a new ideal. I persuaded myself I had much to live for. I had three sons. I became eager to live, to accomplish something worthwhile, something of which my three boys would be proud. This is still the dominant motive of my life.

I could not shake off the lure of the Klondyke. My thoughts were continually of that vast new rugged country, its stark and splendid mountains, its lordly Yukon River, with all its streams and deep blue lakes, its midnight sun, its gold and green of summer, its never-ending dark of winter, illumined by golden stars and flaming northern lights. What I wanted was not shelter and safety, but liberty and opportunity.   ⋙

Chapter IX
BACK TO THE YUKON

A s the days went on, with the straining impatience of a prisoner, I waited for the letter telling me of my investments, of my Klondyke placer diggings. It came in June. The Klondyke had not failed me. As soon as I could, accompanied by Warren, a boy of 12 years of age, I was speeding to the North. Father not only sent me with his backing and blessing, but made plans to follow with Mother, Donald, and Lyman next year, to bring in machinery for a saw and quartz mill.

In the interim I formed a claim-working partnership with two men, and established myself at Gold Hill, a mining camp near Dawson. We built a cabin, storehouse, and bunkhouse for a crew of

YUKON ARCHIVES

Martha Louise managed two sawmills near Dawson. With logs pouring in on the river and two crews to keep track of, she proved herself a true sourdough.

16 men who worked for us. It wasn't a life of leisure for me, as I did the cooking for the entire party. Most of our provisions were still in dried form, and I racked my brains to make the meals tasty and nourishing. I did my own washing and that of Warren as well as the cleaning. I am the type of housekeeper who likes to get most of the housework done in the morning, so I arose at five o'clock. We had the big meal in the middle of the day, after which I took a short nap, arranged a simple supper, and had the evening free to read, talk business, or write in a journal I started, and which I have kept ever since—36 years.

In 1901, true to their promise, my family came in, Father bringing the first two-stamp Tremaine Prospecting Mill, a sawmill, and a hydraulic monitor. The two mills were set up on the left bank of the Klondyke River, about a mile from Dawson, on 30 acres of land, the surface rights of which we purchased from the Canadian Government. The hydraulic outfit was installed at Excelsior Creek, where I had staked my first claims when I came over the Trail of '98. We also built a beautiful six-room cabin which we called "Mill Lodge," a number of one-room cabins, and an assay office. When Father and the family left next year they took Warren with them, and father Purdy entered him in the Junior Department of Notre Dame. Father made me the manager of the mills.

The fall and winter passed uneventfully, but toward spring there was trouble with the mill hands, the chief complaint of my foreman, Brockman, being that he wasn't "goin' to be run by a skirt." This was brought to a head because I had spoken to him about the careless throwing around of the mill tools, peevies, wrenches, wheelbarrows, and other equipment. Being a person who likes order in all things, I did not think I was unreasonable. I felt it was just as easy, when finished with a tool, to put it in its proper place. Our wages and working hours were identical with those of other mills. I had the right to expect the usual efficiency of mill workmen. When I first spoke to him I expected that he would agree with me and see to it that the workmen were more careful. To my surprise he growled, "You rich folks is always grouchin' and pinchy. Ain't you got a whole storehouse full of tools?"

Not trusting myself to say anything at the moment, I walked away. I was very anxious to avoid all trouble as it was the beginning of the summer season; logs were pouring in from up-river almost faster than they could be handled. I had all that I could do with the supervising, and checking in and out of two mill crews, as well as the checking of logs coming in and timber going out. I had also taken over the selling end, as my only salesman had to be let out because of drunkenness. Night after night I was up until two and three o'clock, scaling and seeing that loads left the yard. I was at work again by seven.

I talked the matter over with Donald, a lad only nine years of age, but unusually practical. I asked him to see that all the tools were put in their proper places every night. Matters were not satisfactory, and although I could point to nothing definite, I knew my men were not giving me their best service. I did not want to find fault or nag without good reason. One morning, as I was returning to my cabin, I picked up a hammer, a little farther on an oil can, then a wrench. Donald evidently had not made a clean-up, which surprised me as he was a loyal little worker, especially when interested. I asked him about it at breakfast time.

"I have always put everything away at night, but sometimes lately I have had to put lots of tools away twice," he answered.

So that was it; I was up against deliberate trouble-making.

Before the mill started up I called Brockman into my office. I explained quietly that I was working for others just as he was; that I would like the men to be more careful about putting away tools; that only that morning one of the iron wheelbarrows had been found under the brush in the slough back of the mill.

"I'm sick of bein' ordered about by a damn skirt, and I'm through," he said angrily as he walked away, a string of oaths fairly making the air blue.

"Very well, I will make up your time, and you can come and get your cheque," I called after him.

While doing this I heard a shuffling of feet. On looking up I saw the whole crew but one, headed by Brockman, facing me. "If you don't take back what you said about us bein' careless of tools and shirkin' on the job," he spat at me in a most impudent manner, "we'll all leave now, and that'll close down your little old tin-pot mill this season."

With sinking heart but indifferent manner, I asked each in turn if he agreed with Brockman, and received in reply a sullen "yes" or a shamefaced nod. "Very well. I'm sorry to see men act so foolishly, but there is nothing for me to do but let you go. I am responsible for this property, and men who will not do their duty cannot remain on the place." Then, calling Donald, I said to him, "Go to the mill with these men while they get together their belongings, then come back with them and their cheques will be ready."

Brockman started to talk, but I stood up, looked him squarely in the eye, and said, "You have your cheque. Get out of here and never set foot on this property again."

The men came back shortly. Some seemed inclined to talk, but I refused to listen.

"Where's Ed?" I asked, and was handed a shingle on which was scrawled roughly, "please send my pay by Jack. Sgnd. Ed." This was done. So Ed hadn't the nerve to face me—to stay with me, or to stand out against me.

It was the height of the busy season. Another raft of logs was due immediately. Orders were coming in beyond my fondest hopes, and here we were closed down. I was discouraged, exhausted, and near tears. I might have given in too, when I felt a pat on my shoulder. That nine-year-old boy of mine was saying, "Never mind, mother, I'll work for you."

In a few minutes we were in the mill, banking the fires. Looking up, I saw Sergeant Smith of the Mounted Police, and asked quickly, "What's the matter?"

"That's what I came here to find out. The O.C. sent me. One of your men has just been to the barracks to tell us you might need some help."

It was Ed, I thought; a decent kid after all. Didn't have the nerve to come out in the open but was not going to see any real harm done.

I told the sympathetic sergeant my story; that at the moment I didn't need his help; that I was going to town to rustle another gang, and if I did need help I'd phone the barracks. Smith, however, insisted on leaving a man at the place while I went to Dawson.

Early in the morning, about two, when the last load of sluice-box lumber had left the yard (during the summer months in Yukon the heavy hauling is always done at night, when the rays of the sun are not so fiercely hot), Donald and I again carefully banked the fires and a sleepy boy and his tired mother were eating a few sandwiches before turning in. Looking out of the window I caught sight of a man going into the mill, bending over as he walked. We ran out, but the intruder was nowhere to be found. Next morning everything at the mill seemed as usual, and we decided that the late-caller was probably one of the former workmen returning to get something he had left in his hasty departure the day before.

The news of my labour troubles soon spread throughout the country, and within three days I had a complete crew and was ready to start up again. Brockman did everything in his power to prevent men from working for me, but they only laughed at his efforts.

All was in readiness to start. "Let 'er go easy, boys!" called my new foreman, Dandy Smith. There was a whir of wheels, followed by a sudden rending splitting noise. The little engine was running wild. In a second the power was turned off. We all stood looking at one another in wonder, until brought to our senses by hearing Dandy say, "Damn the man!" A hurried examination showed the trouble. The bearing caps on the main drive shaft had been loosened and the bearings and oil cups filled with steel filings. Had the machinery been going full tilt it would have been ruined, and the whole summer's business lost.

We notified the police at once. All former employees were questioned, and all, save Brockman, who was living alone in a cabin not far from the mill, were able to give satisfactory accounts of themselves. He might have been the prowler we had seen two nights before, but I could never prove it. He made so many threats of "getting me" that the men finally informed the police, who told him he'd better get out of the country by "the downriver path."

He obeyed (as everybody did an order from the Mounties). Later I was told, as he shoved his boat from the wharf, he shouted back, "I'll get that hellcat yet!"

I heard that when he landed on American soil the sheriff was waiting for him, and took him into custody to answer a charge of long standing.

It was during the winter of 1901 when I was still running the sawmill that Dawson's first and only holdup occurred—one 60-below-zero January night at two o'clock. A heavy fog hung over the town like a soft grey blanket. Electric lights blinked suddenly at passers-by and as quickly winked out. Now and then footsteps crunched through the snow with ghostly sounds. Front Street, usually teeming with the night life of the dance halls, saloons, gambling joints, was deserted. The terrific cold had driven most of the night-hawks to their cabins.

Listlessly the dealer at the roulette table in the old Dominion Saloon rolled the little black ball without a bet being made. Black-jack dealers were making phony bets with the boosters, who sat around waiting for suckers who failed to appear. A few miners lounged at the bar, buying occasional drinks for the dance hall girls, who crowded about the huge Klondyke stove, which blazed and roared until its sides were a dull red.

Suddenly the rear door of the saloon was flung open. Swiftly and silently two masked men stepped into the room. "Hands up!" shouted the taller of the two, as he and his companion covered the company with a Winchester rifle and a Colt six-shooter. Amazed, there was nothing to do but obey. Swiftly the smaller of the two bandits emptied the cash drawer of the bar, the tills of the gambling tables, and went through the pockets of the victims. The women, frightened and whimpering, huddled together. One screamed as the short bandit approached them. "Another yap out of you," he said with an ugly gesture of the Colt revolver, "and you'll never roll another sucker. Come through, and be quick about it."

The job finished, the holdup men backed to the door, the leader threatening, "I'll croak the first damn one of you who moves," and then they disappeared into the fog as silently as they had come.

Simultaneously the first holdup victims leaped into action. The Mounted Police were informed, and the manhunt was on. The desperadoes had the advantage of the fog as well as a few minutes' start. To make a clean getaway they would have to travel either up-trail to the coast, or down-trail to Alaska—a new trail was certain death.

The police at both boundaries were warned immediately by wire. It was impossible to send much of a description of the men, as their faces had been completely masked and they had worn ordinary clothes with no distinguishing marks. The one point of agreement was that one was tall, the other short. Indignation was general, for violation of the law under the Canadian flag, indeed under the very noses of the Red Coats, was unheard of. It wasn't good form. It simply wasn't done. The thieves had no friends or sympathizers in the whole town.

A house-to-house search was instituted at once, and within a couple of days a tall, bland, baby-faced man named Tommerlin, who could not give a satisfactory account of his whereabouts the night of the holdup, was held by the Mounties. (It was acknowledged that their efforts were considerably assisted by information given by a dashing brunette.)

Under the promise of partial immunity from punishment, Tommerlin turned King's evidence, confessed he was implicated, and surrendered his share of the loot. He said he was one of a band of three, the others being Harris and Brophy. Harris had planned the whole thing to the minutest detail, but at the last minute had lost his nerve and wouldn't go through with it.

Disgust at the lack of loyalty of his companions undoubtedly excited the sympathy of the public for Brophy, the little bandit in some hide-out. Double-crossing a partner is not "playing the game" in the North, or as Robert Service has aptly put it, "A promise made is a debt unpaid, and the trail has its own stern code." Many were heard to say openly that they hoped Brophy would never be captured. There were strong expressions of disapproval of Tommerlin, who had sold out to save himself. This might have had something to do with the fact that the search for Brophy went on fruitlessly for months.

One morning as I was finishing the breakfast dishes I heard the door creak (we never locked our doors in the old days). Turning round I saw a bullet-headed little man peering into the room and casting suspicious glances about.

"Are you alone?" he asked in a voice hardly above a whisper.

"Yes. Come in. Close the door."

He stealthily closed it, then opened it quickly and started to back out as Donald came into the room.

"I thought you said you were alone."

"Well, I am, except for this child. What's the matter with you? What do you want?"

"Food. Only food. I haven't had anything to eat for three days."

I had plenty of that. There was cold ham, muffins, and coffee left over from breakfast. It took only a few minutes to warm the coffee, and the stranger was soon devouring wolfishly.

Fascinated, Donald watched him. "Are you very poor? Can't you get work? Where did you come from? Where are you going?" he asked, almost in one breath, as children do.

"Donald, get at your lessons," I said peremptorily, before the man could answer.

From the moment of his entrance, his stealthy manner, his

evident fear of meeting anyone, aroused my suspicions that he might be Brophy, the much-hunted bandit. I wanted to get rid of him, yet I didn't want to give him up. Without further word I did up a parcel of bread, butter, ham, tea, and sugar, and, handing it to him, said, "I am not sure who you are, and I don't want to know. But now that you are warm and well fed, take my advice and mush on."

With a grateful "thank you," and a look that haunted me for several days, he went out.

Late that night a loud knock at my door brought me to my feet with a jump out of bed. Hastily donning a wrapper and slippers I opened it, to see a Mounted Policeman. Looking around, he said, "I take it you have no strangers here." By this time Donald, in wide-eyed amazement, was standing beside me. He asked for the keys to the assay office and quartz mill, which I promptly handed over. While we were awaiting his return, Donald snuggled up very closely to me and whispered, "Mother, will they get the man?"

"What man, son?"

"The poor little man you fed."

"Who do you think he is, Donald?"

"Brophy, the holdup man, Mother. He stayed in our old Carmichael cabin two nights, and I heard some men at Gilkers talking about him. But I won't tell. It was mean of that old, fat Tommerlin to tell on him. He was a coward."

Marvelling at the child's sympathy and understanding, I was wondering what I would say when the policeman returned, especially if he should question me.

But he didn't. As he handed me my keys he warned, "Better keep your doors locked at all hours. A tough character has been seen hanging around this neighbourhood."

Shortly Brophy was captured at the Old Stockade Roadhouse on Bonanza Creek. He had been my visitor. He was tried, found guilty, and given a life sentence. Harris got 10 years' hard labour, while Tommerlin, the informer, was deported to the United States territory, from whence he came.

Brophy, absolutely refused to divulge the hiding-place of his share of the loot, several thousand dollars in gold dust. Possibly someday some lucky person will discover the cache of jewellery, money, and gold dust, or maybe it will remain where it was hidden until the end of time. ⟡

Chapter X
DAWSON SETTLES DOWN

I shall always remember the first three years of the present century—years which passed so quickly that, when a weekly mail service was established in Dawson, I had not been conscious of the need of it. Of course it was not all easy going, and there were times of "tough sledding," but there were no tragedies. I liked the life, the vigorous challenge of it—the work and play of it. I had faith in myself—that this tide in the affairs of my life would lead me on to fortune. My first claims proved to be rich—real pay dirt. If only I had had the sense to cash in on them I should be wealthy today. Instead, I bought other claims . . . grubstaked men . . . but why tell the old, old story?

I had indeed made a new life for myself. Except for my relatives I was entirely out of touch with Chicago friends and associations. I applied for my divorce—received it with no difficulty—and with what meant more to me than all else, the unanimous approval of my family. I had Donald and Lyman with me, the former going to public school, the latter, when he was four, to an excellent kindergarten. I had a capable French housekeeper, wife of the mill watchman.

Donald received the most expert teaching in the Dawson public school, as the finest teachers from every part of Canada sought the chance of going to Yukon, because of the large salaries and adventurous atmosphere.

Father Purdy had persuaded me to allow him to take full responsibility for Warren, and he had now entered him at Annapolis, Maryland.

The sawmill made me plenty of money. I was continually sending for furniture and other things, which I selected from Eaton's and Simpson's catalogues, to make Mill Lodge more comfortable and attractive. I was able to buy the most beautiful clothes—a yearly Paris gown from Madame Aubert, who visited the world's centre of fashion annually to choose the loveliest and latest creations for the

Third Avenue in Dawson about 1901. Perhaps Martha Louise felt a touch of sympathy for the Chicago Hotel's homesick owners.

women of Dawson, who thought nothing in those days of paying $500 for a gown. I also ordered many clothes from White's in Woodstock, Ontario. I sent my exact measurements, a photograph, and a description of my colouring. They sent me a princess slip, which they asked to have fitted by a local dressmaker, and samples of various silks and woollen suitings, and style books. I used to step right into these clothes—the results never failing to live up to the fashion sheet pictures.

My business brought me in touch with all kinds of people. I recall one young woman who was one of my customers. She ran a questionable boardinghouse. She and her boarders were arrested on the usual charge of selling liquor without a licence. Their lawyer advised them to plead guilty and pay the customary $50 fine. After the usual question of "Guilty or not guilty?" to the consternation of the court she broke out with a fine scorn, "Me plead guilty? Why should I plead guilty, when half the men in this town . . . ."

She started pointing to individuals in the courtroom but the judge stopped her. There was a hurried adjournment of the case, and it was only the fear of the blue ticket which made her finally plead guilty.

One time she came to me with a pathetic story. She had had a letter from her mother, saying she was coming to visit and was bringing her grandson. "My own little boy," she added confidentially. "Saturday and Sunday are apt to be wild days at my place; and will you help me and ask them to visit you weekends? I'll pay you anything you want," she said.

"Oh, I couldn't make money that way," I answered quickly. She turned away, all the misery of the world in her eyes.

"But wait, you haven't let me finish. Why not rent one of my mill cabins for your mother and son? Your little fellow can play with my boys, and I'll see that your mother has plenty to do over the weekend."

"God bless you! God bless you!" she said as she walked away, the tears running down her face.

As the gold dust grew less plentiful the wild frontier life of Dawson's stampede days subdued. No longer were there miners who thought nothing of a thousand dollars a night for champagne, who "set 'em up" round after round. Convivial celebrations still continued to be popular, and were particularly rampant over the New Year. Some of the early day party songs of sourdoughs are recalled almost in the light of traditions at their present-day gatherings. The man who had "never refused a drink since 1882" was only beginning to be in good form when he had the urge to sing "The Harp that once through Tara's Halls." The Scotsman insisted on "Loch Lomond," the Irishman, "Killarney," and the Frenchman, "Alouette," while one now nationally known sourdough claimed exclusive singing rights to "Annie Laurie."

They did the most ridiculous things. Once they tied the doorknob of a very nervous hotel resident to another doorknob across the hall. They then let loose a cat and dog in the corridor. Hearing the wild commotion both occupants rushed to their doors, tugged frantically, each closing more securely the door across the hall.

Several men made pathetic efforts to set up homes. One man, after living with a girl for many years, decided to marry her. He had struck it rich, and they were going to do it in style. They had Madame Aubert send to Paris for a wedding gown, which came over the trail carefully packed in a zinc-lined box, the express alone amounting to $150.

There was plenty of good wholesome fun—dancing being the

favourite winter diversion, and many a good time I had at "Honour yer pardners all! Grand right and left."

The big social event of the season, as the society editors would say, was the annual ball of the Arctic Brotherhood—membership in it being the most coveted and greatest honour that could befall a sourdough, as he had to prove that he had been "inside the watershed prior to the first day of July 1897." This fraternity built the A.B. Hall, one of the finest buildings in the country, the hardwood for the floor being imported at an enormous cost.

And what an orchestra! Herr Freimuth, the leader, was a graduate violinist of the Conservatory of Leipzig; Signor Lopez, the cornet soloist, had played at the Royal Opera House, Madrid; Telgmann had been first clarinet in the Boston Symphony Orchestra, other members each having attained some musical distinction.

What a colourful assemblage! The Mounted Police in their brilliant uniforms, the women in their magnificent Paris gowns, and the members of the Brotherhood and other sourdoughs (mostly men of magnificent physique) in the most formal "black and white," even white kid gloves, quite evidently not comfortable but definitely very proper.

At these affairs might be seen such men as Commissioner William Ogilvie, the second Governor of the Yukon, one of the straightest men who ever staked a claim, an explorer, prospector, untiring land surveyor, and good fellow. He was better at finding gold than keeping it. It is certain that he could have had the famous Bonanza fraction, generally conceded as the richest piece of ground for its size in the world, discovered by Dick Lowe, who was surveying for him at the time. Ogilvie let Lowe take it, and he washed out of it over $700,000 of gold dust in six weeks.

It was at an A.B. ball that Alex MacDonald, the "Big Moose," sometimes called "King of the Klondyke," introduced to Dawson his young and beautiful wife. MacDonald was one who struck it rich—his pack train sometimes bringing from his claims sacks of gold dust worth $300,000.

I think of other personalities who added to the gaiety of these occasions. Joe Boyle, to go down in history as "Saviour of Roumania," "Duff" Pattullo, to become Premier of British Columbia, "Foxy" Grandpa Walsh, later Governor of Alberta. Walsh was a lawyer and a fine scout. He ran for Mayor of Dawson, but was defeated by a saloon keeper, Jimmy McDonald, which induced the Commissioner's secretary, "Clemmie" Burns (later Supreme Court Librarian, Ottawa), to remark, "That's how much the mob appreciates real worth."

There were two Pattullos in the North—"T.D.," the younger, became the Premier of British Columbia. He was in the Government service, resigned, and went into the brokerage business. His elder brother, "J.D.," was a King's Counsellor, and was affectionately known as "Pat" by his familiars. The Pattullo family also played important parts in the early gold rush days of British Columbia, and an uncle of the two Pattulo boys struck it rich on Williams Creek, in the Cariboo gold rush of the '60's.

Another popular winter diversion was skating and ice carnivals. I remember a bitter controversy waged over the matter of allowing the dance hall girls to buy season tickets to the new rink. The final decision was in the affirmative, this accompanied by an emphatic warning that if any girl were caught smoking or using profane language in the ladies' dressing-room her ticket would be forfeited. The fancy dress carnivals were equal to and even surpassed those in other parts of the world. There was every kind of costume from "Night" (long black dress with silver paper stars), "Day" (blue dress with gold suns) and "Bowery Girls" to "Fairy Queens."

Odd evenings were filled in with card parties—progressive whist, euchre, and 500, and bridge whist was introduced at this time. Poker never went out of fashion, and, as in stampede days, all-day and -night games are a part of Yukon life today.

In summer tennis was the chief women's sport, the long light making play possible until 10 or 11. We organized "mixed" tournaments, which added teas, suppers, and dances to our social life.

Sometimes we women sourdoughs like to boast how popular we were with the menfolk. But again I owe it to the girls of today to admit that we did not have the competition they have. Indeed, in those days, we single women, with homes in which to entertain, were so few that our number could be counted on the fingers of one hand, and I don't think it would take all the fingers. Scarcely a fortnight passed that I did not have a proposal of marriage. If I missed I thought that I was falling off and getting old. I've had a number of men tell me they "couldn't live without me," but most of these men are alive today, all happily married with families. ❊

※

Chapter XI
I BECOME MRS. GEORGE BLACK

One day it became necessary for me to consult a lawyer as one of my mill hands had bought goods for himself and charged them to me. George Black, of an old New Brunswick family, a sourdough, who had caught the gold fever and had come to the country in 1897, was recommended. I liked him at once. He was good-looking and clever. As we talked I learned he was interested in politics, and had a sincere desire to serve the Yukon—to devote himself to the development and tremendous possibilities of this great, rich part of Canada.

I invited him to my home. The affairs of human beings move quickly in the North, and within two weeks he proposed. I was not eager to marry again, yet I liked him more than any man I knew. He was attractive, serious, and a good companion. He was an outdoor man, a real sportsman, and a lover of nature. From the beginning he was interested in my boys, and won them completely.

He always included them in our outdoor expeditions. Together we studied the birds, canoed, and tramped far and wide as he photographed our feathered friends—with fine results. We learned their migratory habits, followed their flights, and there is no finer place in all the world to see the birds at their best than the valley of the Yukon, especially in the spring, when they have their new and beautiful dresses, are ready to make love, go housekeeping, and raise a family.

What wonderful times we had! So fond did the boys become of our new friend that they began to ask, "Mother, when are you going to marry Mr. Black?" and I would answer, "Did George Black give you two bits today?"

For once in my life I let my head govern my heart. It took me two years to make up my mind.

We were married on August 1, 1904, at my home, Mill Lodge; my husband's parents, his uncle, his brother, and my boys and a very few dear friends being present at the wedding.

My wedding dress, made by Redfern, New York, was a very beautiful creation of pearl-grey velvet, and I laugh to myself now as I recall it. The floor-length skirt, lined with blush-pink silk, was gathered into a 16-inch yoke, with rows and rows of shirring, and fell in a short train. The high-necked bodice was fashioned with a lace yoke over blush-pink silk, the leg-o'-mutton sleeves being trimmed with lace and pink silk piping, fastened tightly at the wrist. I carried a "granny muff" of flat pink roses, with long loops of pale pink ribbon reaching almost to the floor, while cosily nestled among the roses were three small birds, one white, one pink, and one pale lemon. I wore a merry widow hat made entirely

Returning after many years, Mr. and Mrs. George Black stand in the doorway of their first home, a six-room cabin called Mill Lodge, a mile from Dawson.

of pink roses, the brim raised at the left side and three little birds like those on the muff reposing under it. It all sounds too ridiculous now, but at the time the outfit was considered very swanky.

Among other dresses in my trousseau was a white panne velvet made in princess style, low on the shoulders, and finished with a fichu of real lace, which had trimmed Mother's wedding gown. I shall never forget wearing it for the first time at the "Bal Poudre" in Dawson, that winter of 1904. I had powdered my hair, built it high on my head with innumerable puffs, and made up my face with rouge and black court plaster patches. An old-fashioned tiny lace fan that had belonged to Grandmother Munger was the finishing touch. As I entered the hall, Madame Bergholz, mother of United States consul in Dawson, sitting next to Mrs. Wood, wife of Col. Z. T. Wood, O.C. North West Mounted Police in Yukon, said, "What a beautiful woman! Who is she?" and, receiving the reply, "Mrs. George Black," remarked, "Impossible! I've known her for years." Mrs. Wood thought the joke too good to keep from me.

Early in the fall we moved from Mill Lodge into Dawson. From that time on life seemed to flow as easily and normally as it does with the average married couples. The boys loved their new father. Lyman, only 5, immediately called himself Lyman Black, and later, when he enlisted, asked his stepfather if this might be legalized, permission being gladly given.

No father could have guided or trained young boys better than George Black. He taught them to handle a canoe, make camp, shoot, and fish. He was a real chum with them. I shall never cease to be grateful to him for his guidance of the physical, mental, and moral training of my sons at an age when every boy needs a father.

I am a firm believer in the principle that married couples, from the beginning, should be in complete harmony in religion, in country, and in politics. So immediately after my marriage, without compunction, I became an Anglican, an Imperialist, and a Conservative. Not only did I become a member of the Anglican Church, but I took an active part in the Women's Auxiliary, later being elected president, which position I held for a number of years.

I am an average Christian, but as a child there had been so much compulsory going to church, Sunday school, and prayer meeting that today I am sometimes neglectful about going to church. Mother continually impressed upon us that if we followed the golden rule we would be acceptable in God's sight—and I believe that.

The pioneers of the church in the North had gruelling tasks before them, and on the honour rolls of intrepid missionaries will ever be the names of those whom I shall always be proud to call my friends—Bishops Bompas, Stringer, Rowe, and their wives; Father Judge, Archdeacon Stuck, and the Sisters of Ste. Anne, who today are carrying on their work of mercy, begun in the North by their Order over half a century ago.

They came, these men and women of God, not at the call of gold or greed, not with visions of accumulated fortunes and things of earth, but in the great cause of their Master—to save souls. With no sparing of self, they braved the cruelties of the country, brought hope to the hopeless, faith to the faithless, and comfort to the sick and dying. That was their mission and that was their reward.

Until I married George Black I had little knowledge of Canadian politics, but I learned from him that almost coincident with the discovery of gold in the Klondyke, in 1896, there had come a change in federal government, that, after 18 years in opposition, the Liberals had come into power. They hailed this new El Dorado as a God-given opportunity to place many of the eager office and job seekers—the usual camp followers of political upheavals. Then, as now, it was, "To the victor belongs the spoils."

At first the government had been in the hands of the North West Mounted Police, and administered by Major Thomas Morro Walsh, who had established Fort Walsh in the Cypress Hills in the '70's, and who lived up to the highest traditions of the force in establishing law and order. Well they fulfilled their task. They made short shrift of the criminal element, in marked contrast to the lawlessness of Alaska.

In August 1898, by Dominion Act of Parliament, the Yukon Territory was created. It comprised a tract of land, over 200,000 square miles, that portion of the North-West Territories bounded on the north by the Arctic Ocean, south by the Province of British Columbia, east by the height of land between the Yukon and Mackenzie rivers and west by Alaska. This Yukon Act (the constitution of the Yukon Territory today) provided for the establishment of a territorial government consisting of a Commissioner, appointed by the Dominion Government, a position similar to that of lieutenant-governor, and an appointed council of

YUKON ARCHIVES

JAMES WHYARD

Government House, the official residence of the commissioner of Yukon Territory was marvelously ornate — a splendid example of "contractor's art." Following a fire in 1906, it was remodeled in a somewhat colonial style.

10, inclusive of the chief officials of the Territory—the Gold Commissioner, Senior Judge of the Territorial Court, Registrar of Land Titles, Comptroller, and Officer Commanding North West Mounted Police. (Major Walsh was appointed the first Commissioner, or governor.)

The administration of criminal law continued to be by the North West Mounted Police—sound, swift, relentless, and effective; but that of civil affairs, under the government of the day, reeked with graft and crookedness, and will ever be a blot on Yukon history.

Establishing this first civil government meant the letting of numerous contracts for erection of public buildings—post offices, courthouses, administration buildings, and an elaborate government house at Dawson.

This offical residence, situated on a prominent site at the confluence of the rivers, was a splendid example of "contractor's art," and was one of the sights of the country. It was ornate to the superlative degree, loaded with fancy fretwork of fantastic design. On either side of the third storey were large boxlike ornaments, which in these early days were derisively called "ballot boxes," in reference to alleged ballot box frauds. (Following a fire, 1905, the house was remodelled somewhat after the colonial style.)

Commissioner James Hamilton Ross (third commissioner) was the first to live in Government House. He brought his wife and family, and after a brief time Mrs. Ross with their little daughter and niece left on the *Islander* for the outside to buy the remaining furnishings for the official residence. This ship, loaded heavily with thousands of dollars of gold dust, struck a rock near Juneau, and Mrs. Ross and family were among those drowned. Commissioner Ross was ill for many months, many fearing he would not survive the shock of this tragedy. He left Dawson, and while outside was elected the first Yukon member of the Canadian Parliament.

I often used to walk by Government House and deplore that only the prosperous and important were entertained there. I wished that its doors were thrown wider open to the real makers of Yukon—miners, prospectors, and others who had sacrificed so much and had so few comforts or lovely possessions. Little did I think the time would come when I should see this wish fulfilled and I, as chatelaine, would have the power to carry it out.

In 1902 the Territory was given the privilege of electing a member to the Dominion Parliament, with full right not only to sit and speak in the House of Commons, but to vote, this differing from that of the Alaskan representative in Congress, who had no vote.

My husband told me that the flagrant corruption of the first election was the worst in the political history of the country. Numbers of foreigners were railroaded through a fake form of naturalization and allowed to vote. In some instances these foreigners were totally ignorant of the fraud, and did not discover until later years that they had been duped. Credulous hotelkeepers gave government supporters large credits on I.O.U.'s or "tabs," as they were called then. After the election these were repudiated and unredeemed, and the party responsible and its followers nicknamed "Tabs."

In one transaction the agent who went to Skagway with money to hire pluggers, lost his roll at the roulette wheel and had neither money nor tabs to pay the carload of imported aliens who, in the meantime, had voted. When they found that the agent had skipped the country, in their rage they smashed train windows, tore up seats, and raised general ruction. It was said that for years he dared not appear within miles of Skagway. So complete was the frame-up among the higher-ups that these election frauds were beyond the law.

Ballot boxes were stuffed. Polls at which there were not over 30 or 40 inhabitants returned boxes containing hundreds of ballots.

Flushed with victory the political ring carried on with a high hand. My own mining activities brought me into close touch with their administration in this respect, and I was indignant at the gross injustice and dishonesty of it. Huge concessions of mining land compared to claims staked by prospectors and miners were given to political favourites. This prevented development, and in some instances these lands were unworked for years. Miners were cheated out of claims by the merest subterfuges, or by falsifying of records. It was a common experience for a man who had staked a claim on a distant creek, after having given a description of it on his application to record, to be told, when he called a few days later, that the claim had already been staked.

Men stood in line for days to reach recorders' wickets, while the favoured used the "side door." Similarly at the post office, the long customary wait could be shortened by an investment of $10 and up.

Intoxicating liquors could be imported into the Territory only by permission of the federal Minister of the Interior. Again government favourites obtained permits, and brought these in by the boatload and sold them at fabulous prices.

Indignation meetings were held, resolutions and protests were drafted, delegations sent to Ottawa. But communication was so slow, and direct evidence so hard to produce at a distance of 4,000 miles, that nothing was done.

Came the news of the Treadgold concession, this surpassing all others in flagrancy. Under its terms, all claims lapsing in the Klondyke area reverted to the concessionaire. It had been put over at Ottawa. Such a storm of indignation followed that the matter became serious, and the government cancelled it and appointed a commission, headed by Judge Britton of Ontario, to investigate these alleged illegal methods of obtaining concessions, their evil effects on the mining industry, and the injustice to the individual miners.

At one of the sittings of the commission, Judge Britton threatened to commit a witness, who had been using strong language, for contempt of court. To the judge's surprise the miner pointed out that as a member of the commission he had no power to do this, and besides, "the whole damn thing was beneath contempt."

The year of our marriage, 1904, the country was in the throes of another bitter election campaign. The local Liberals were divided into two camps, the notorious "Tabs" and "Steam-beers," so named because their leader was the president of a brewing company. The latter joined the Conservatives to form an "Independent" party, and nominated Dr. Alfred Thompson—an erstwhile Nova Scotian, a pioneer physician, always ready to answer the call of sickness at any time, any distance, and in any weather—to oppose the leader of the Tabs. George was working tooth and nail for Dr. Thompson.

A local newspaper disclosed a Tab plot to win the election. This was to post voters' lists for public inspection a short time before election day, and later to revise them, striking off enough names of opposing voters to guarantee their victory.

There ensued a terrific row. It was open season for hunting enumerators. A committee of two well-known citizens was appointed to get in touch with the senior judge of the Territory who had appointed the enumerators. The returning officer was rounded up. An angry and excited mob followed the three down the street.

Suddenly a rope was produced and the crowd seized the ashen-faced, trembling returning officer and quickly slipped it round his neck, to the cries of "String him up! String him up!" They were about to do it on the nearest telegraph pole, but the committee prevented it. A number of enumerators with their lists fled to the Mounted Police barracks for protection from the now thoroughly aroused public. For weeks a guard of Mounted Police patrolled the residence of the nervous senior judge.

The combined "Steam-beers" and Tories elected Dr. Thompson with a big majority. The back of the ring was broken.

As my husband was going in for a political career, I stood ready to do my womanly bit to help him. This meant cooking meals for his supporters and attending political meetings. In the ensuing years he was elected to the Yukon Council three times, once by acclamation.

With the passing years my political enthusiasm grew. I recall attending an election meeting at the A.B. Hall, when George, as a council candidate, was one of the speakers. As he arose, the woman next to me said, "They'll never let that man speak!"

"That man will speak if he stands there till hell freezes over. I'm his wife, and I know he won't be scared away by any damn bunch of hoodlums," I said. That silenced her. George did speak, while I and others cheered to the roof.

Every election night we were at home to our friends, supporters and non-supporters, who were invited by a newspaper notice. From 200 to 400 came—to rejoice or commiserate. I prepared for two days—cooked hams, chickens, and turkeys for real "he-man" sandwiches. I'd hate to offer a sourdough a plate of decorated, one-bite, open-faced sandwiches of today's fashion. I could never survive his dirty look! I made gallons of salads, dozens of cakes, and quarts of punch, "wet" and "dry."

As a member of the Yukon Council my husband introduced and piloted through the Miners' and Woodmen's Lien Ordinances. Prior to this it was a common occurrence for miners and woodmen to work all winter and not get a dollar's wages. This was due to the fact that employers often financed camp supplies and equipment by mortgages or credit, and the entire output of gold and wood could be seized by mortgagees and creditors—leaving the workmen nothing—not even the price of the next meal. Thanks to George Black, today wages have the first lien on production. ❈

Chapter XII
DAWSON ON THE WANE

Happy years, especially in retrospect, flash by. George Black and I were eminently suited to each other—each interested in and promoting the other's special pursuits. I liked the municipal and federal political activity that centred about our home; being in the know of the who and why of political nominees of our party and the plans of election campaign; and later their wild excitement. (No election campaign in Yukon is ever mild.) We both enjoyed splendid health and had a host of friends—always welcome at any meal to take pot luck with the family. Although not lucky enough to make a clean-up in our mining investments, my husband's law business provided a good income, and each year we added some new treasure to our comfortable home. We had our two growing boys, sturdy and full of life, keeping us young with them.

Donald and Lyman were average boys of their age, not over studious, had a fine scorn for dressing up, were addicts of "cupboard love," and deep into sport, pranks, and fights.

It was my custom to gather as many "homeless" for Christmas dinner as our house could accommodate, and one hectic Yuletide holiday (1905) stands out clearly in my memory. We had decorated our tree on Christmas Eve, and then, as usual, gone to midnight Mass at the Roman Catholic church. Arriving home, we looked upon a scene of complete devastation. Our pup had pulled down the tree, torn open parcels, and was still hard at it. We set up the tree, aroused the proprietor of the store which sold decorations, and it was well on to morning before we had restored order and filled the boys' stockings, our lights in the meantime attracting numerous friends, who became more convivial as the hours went by. After putting to bed one who had passed out (in a spare bed in Lyman's room) we ourselves turned in, hoping for a few hours sleep.

I had barely dropped off when I heard a bellow from Lyman's room. When I got there I found our "guest" had come to, was

Mrs. George Black in 1908.

making spitballs and flipping them at Lyman. I was righteously indignant, and expressed it in no uncertain words. But Lyman, once awakened, aroused Donald, and the boys were on the tear to investigate their Christmas presents.

There was no further sleep, so we arose, had breakfast, and went to the Anglican service. We had just settled down to this when the fire-bell rang, and looking from the church window we saw that Government House (two doors away) was on fire. The service was broken up and the whole town turned out to see the fire. It was several hours before I returned home to supervise Christmas dinner, which was another lingering, all-night affair.

Investigation into the Government House fire led to the general belief that it was a case of incendiarism; that there had been a robbery, all traces of which the thief purposed to remove by setting the house afire.

In this connection I had a strange experience. Next spring it was necessary that I should go out to see Father on the business of closing the mill. I took an up-river steamer, and to pass the time away I started palm reading, of which I knew nothing beyond the "heart, fate, and life" lines. A fellow traveller told me that Kennedy, one of the passengers, would like me to read his girl's hand. I turned it aside by saying, "I don't know anything about palm reading." Kennedy sent another message, and so, for want of something better to do, I agreed. I picked up "Swiss Louisa's" hand and told her the usual heart-fate-and-life-line stuff, then added, "Some man, in whom you are deeply interested, will come to a violent end in three—days, months, or years, but it seems very close."

On arrival at Whitehorse three days later the steamer was met by a Mounted Policeman, who arrested Kennedy on the charge of being connected with the Government House robbery and fire. He asked his guard for a drink of water, and with a quick move swallowed a pellet of poison which he had concealed in his coat lapel, and was dead in a few moments. When I got back I was besieged by girls to read their palms—but never again did I dabble in palmistry. You know there is such a thing as quitting while your reputation is good!

Towns and small cities are noted for good times, and Dawson might easily have headed the list. There were teas, receptions, dinner and card parties, and dances, and I must not forget the amateur plays. Ridiculous incidents of these come to me: the finale of a first act when the courtier was kneeling to a queen and was, without warning, struck down by the descending curtain; the heroine holding an empty hand to a warrior saying, "Drink from this goblet, and may its contents infuse your will with new life," and the accompanying stage whisper, "In heaven's name, where's the Scotch?"

Each spring and fall regularly the whole family went camping to shoot or fish. Rolled in our sleeping-bags or fur rugs we slept on bough beds in the open in fine weather, or under canvas or a wickiup (a brush camp built like a lean-to) when it was raining. We did our own cooking, replenishing our larder with the fish we caught, or the wild fowl or big game we shot. Generally we pitched our main camp on the bank of some stream, and from there travelled up and down in our canvas canoes.

On one of these trips I actually shot my first bear. It was not a large bear, nevertheless it was a bear, and I was inordinately proud.

After returning to town a friend was having tea with me. She congratulated me on my accomplishment, and as Donald entered the room, said to him, "Aren't you proud that your mother really killed a bear?"

"Oh, I dunno; it was a mangy old thing that no one else wanted."

His answer was true—the pelt wasn't much good.

We had the privilege of knowing some of the big game hunters who came to Yukon these years, among them Frederick Courtenay Selous, a British explorer of South Africa, ethnologist, and one of the world's most daring hunters. Accompanied by Charles Sheldon, a famous American sportsman, Carl Rungus, a Danish artist, and a party of local hunters, he went up the Macmillan River, where he shot a bull moose with a spread of horns said to be one of the finest in the world. Charles Sheldon gave me a copy of his book, *Wilderness of the Upper Yukon*, and his last book, *The Wilderness of Denali*, published two years after his death, was given to me by his hunting companion, Fenley Hunter, who has been instrumental in the erection of cairns both in Alaska and Yukon to mark spots of historical significance.

In duck-shooting season we were keen to bring down unusual specimens, as my husband was a remarkably clever amateur taxidermist. One spring the boys and I spotted a pair of ducks unlike any we had ever seen. We decided that the boys should carry the canoe some distance up-river, while I, concealed behind some bushes, would remain to signal the location of the ducks. The scheme worked perfectly, with the result that we secured a magnificent pair of king eider ducks, the only ones ever seen in our part of the country, although they are fairly common in the Behring Sea region. We gave these to the Canadian National Museum at

YUKON ARCHIVES

George Black at the end of a successful hunt. Both George and Martha Louise enjoyed hunting, but more as an outing than for the game it provided.

Ottawa. Another spring, quite unexpectedly, a lucky shot brought down a perfect canvas-back duck, a rare kind so far north.

During the summer of 1909 Dawson was on the tiptoe of expectation. For the first time in its history a Governor-General of Canada was to visit Yukon. Word had come that His Excellency Earl Grey, his daughter Lady Sybil, her friend the Honourable Miss Middleton, daughter of Lord Middleton, Lord Lascelles (later the husband of the Princess Royal), and party were coming for a three-day visit in August. Headed by Commissioner Alex Henderson, a committee of government officials and leading citizens made enthusiastic plans for His Excellency's visit—these including trips to near-by mining camps of Bonanza and Eldorado Creek, and two picnics at King Solomon's Dome and in West Dawson.

Chartering a boat the committee met the vice-regal party in mid-stream, some 30 miles above Dawson. His Excellency, his charming daughter, and friend and aides were transferred to the special boat, where a stirring speech of welcome was read by the Commissioner. The party reached Dawson in the evening and went at once to Government House, which had been entirely renovated since the fire, and from which Commissioner Henderson and his wife had moved temporarily to provide suitable quarters for the Governor-General and his suite. Before eight-o'clock breakfast next morning the first question asked by His Excellency of Commissioner Henderson was, "Does Robert Service live far from here?"

"No, only next door."

"I would like to meet him. Send for him to breakfast with us."

This royal recognition of Robert Service, the bank clerk "who wrote verses," had Dawson all agog. Till then Yukoners had not paid much attention to the shy young Scotsman who weighed gold dust and kept the ledgers of the Canadian Bank of Commerce.

The Governor-General gave three dinner-parties at Government House. As George was a member of the council we attended one, and Lord Lascelles was my dinner escort. While His Excellency expressed surprise at the superior type of people he had met in Yukon, and their sophisticated mode of living, I fancied Lord Lascelles was unduly surprised, and gathered that his preconceived idea was that people who chose to live so far from accredited civilization were more or less savages.

Robert Service at his cabin in Dawson City. Dawson took little notice of the bank clerk "who wrote verses" until the visiting Governor-General of Canada asked to meet him. He rarely recited his verses in public.

He was quite concerned that Service had not sent a formal acceptance to his dinner invitation. He took the matter up with "Clemmy" Burns, the Commissioner's secretary. Within an hour Clemmy had "old Alec Ross," the bank messenger (who left $100,000 to his relatives on his death) speeding over with the required *R.S.V.P.* Service more than made up for any omission by presenting Lady Sybil and Hon. Miss Middleton with autographed copies of *Songs of a Sourdough.*

Service was an outstanding example of the Scriptural saying, "A prophet is not without honour, save in his own country." This dreamy modest Scottish bank clerk came to Yukon in 1905 as a ledger keeper in the Canadian Bank of Commerce at Whitehorse, and two years later was transferred to Dawson. The first time I saw him was at an ice carnival, when he represented one of the Gold Dust Twins.

As no one else before or since, he was able to interpret in rhyme the lure of the Northland, the wild raw life of stampede days against Nature's magnificient background. He told in vivid irresistible measure of "The Spell of the Yukon" where:

> *There's gold, and it's haunting and haunting;*
> *It's luring me on as of old;*
> *Yet it isn't the gold that I'm wanting*
> *So much as just finding the gold.*
> *It's the great, big, broad land 'way up yonder.*
> *It's the forests where silence has lease;*
> *It's the beauty that thrills me with wonder,*
> *It's the stillness that fills me with peace.* *

Enclosing a cheque to pay for their publishing, he sent his first poems, *Songs of a Sourdough,* to an Eastern publishing firm. His friends say he was astonished to the degree of "nearly dropping dead" when the publishers returned the cheque and offered to take the risk. And risk it was, thought the publishers at first, until they heard their printers rhyming them off as they were setting them up in type. After this, publication was so rushed that the publishers' salesmen took their orders on galley proofs, which, as they crossed

---

*From *The Collected Poems of Robert Service,* by Robert Service; reprinted with permission of publishers Dodd, Mead & Company, Inc.

the country, they read to fellow travellers on the trains. *Songs of a Sourdough* (published 1907) has gone well over the fortieth edition since and is still a popular record of the early hectic life. . . ."Of those Dawson Days, and the sin and the blaze, and the whole town open wide. . . ."

Soon Service became the vogue in Canada and United States, and the man in the street and professional and non-professional elocutionists recited his rollicking, virile rhymes, especially his narrative poems, "The Shooting of Dan McGrew" and "The Cremation of Sam McGee." It seemed the whole "outside" had discovered this new poet, but at home he was still a nobody.

The new Commissioner (Henderson) came in reciting Service. He was tendered a civic banquet at Whitehorse. One of his first questions was, "Where is Robert Service?" But again the poet had not even been invited. They sent for him, and Commissioner Henderson asked him to recite some of his verses. "Oh, I couldn't without the book," replied the nervous young man. Many thought this was just an excuse to cover up his shyness, but other Yukoners said that Service forgot his poems as soon as they were on paper.

Yet Service did recite his verse in the presence of a few close friends and on one or two rare occasions. I recall one recital which was the talk of the town next day. Clement Burns, secretary of the Dawson Amateur Athletic Society, had invited him as his guest to the association's annual banquet. Service accepted only on the condition that he would not be expected to recite his poems. It was a bitterly cold night in midwinter. The large gymnasium was heated only by two stoves, one at each end of it, and it was like an ice house. Hot Scotches were passed in quick succession to keep the "inner man" warm, even if his exterior were freezing. The company mellowed, and Service, leaning toward the secretary, said, "Burnsie, I have written an unpublished and uncensored poem or so, which I might recite. . . ." "Burnsie" lost no time in getting word to the chairman, and cheers lasting several minutes greeted the announcement. Service recited "Touch the Button, Nell," the story of a poor old faded dance hall girl who had become sodden with liquor, but kept touching the button for still another round. Three parsons hurriedly left the room in complete accord with the publisher who had expurgated this "gem" from the volume.

I recall only one time that Service did appear before the whole public of Dawson, and this was at a charity performance. The only person able to persuade him was Mrs. Sinclair, wife of the Presbyterian minister, a most cultured woman who before her marriage had been an artist on *Punch*.

Service left the bank in 1909, retired to a small log cabin in Dawson (one of today's tourist sights) to write his one and only novel, *The Trail of '98*. This prose work never became as popular as his verses.

At this time the Yukon Government offered a prize of $200 for the best exhibit of native wild flowers. This gave a new impetus to my zeal of many years of studying haunts and habits of our wild flowers. My interest had now become known, and I was asked to speak on this topic at various women's teas, church and sewing meetings. I found my talks more interesting if illustrated, and I began to press and mount flowers—washing in the backgrounds with watercolours. I called this hobby "artistic botany," for in no way do I claim to be a scientific botanist.

I was interested at once in the Government's competition, and set to work arranging an exhibit. I planned it with a three-fold purpose: first, to show as many varieties as possible; second, to stress the scientific angle by mounting whole plants; and third, to demonstrate artistic effects by unusual arrangement.

Friends brought me flowers of every kind. Children combed the hills and valleys for me. Others hearing of my work—rough miners from the creeks—called at my door, sheepishly and tenderly taking from their pockets rare delicate flowers and plants.

I assembled 464 varieties. I made a harp of four-leaf clovers, with strings of the finest grass; "Odd Fellows' " links of canary creeper; and a heart of pink and white immortelles. It was really a beautiful display, and I won the prize.

The exhibit was sent to the World's Fair, which was being held in Seattle that year, and where it did much to disperse the too prevalent idea that Yukon is a barren, frozen land.

The golden days of Dawson began to wane. The gold fever had worn itself out. The population dwindled to 6,000. Law work grew less and George decided we should go outside for a year while he studied for the law examinations of British Columbia.

In 1909 we left for Vancouver, and the next two summers I spent on one of the happiest missions of my life—gathering and mounting wild flowers of the Rocky Mountains for the Canadian Pacific Railway.   ⁂

Chapter XIII

GATHERING WILD FLOWERS FOR A RAILWAY

It was my Yukon wild flower work that was responsible for this commission to gather and mount wild flowers of British Columbia for exhibition purposes in Canadian Pacific Railway stations and hotels.

After we moved to Vancouver, one day I invited to lunch Mrs. Hayter Reed, well known for her work in the interior decorating of Canadian Pacific hotels and chalets, of which her husband was general manager. For place cards I had some wild Yukon pressed flowers, mounted on watercolour paper, with pretty ribbon bows. Mrs. Reed admired them. I told her of my Yukon flower exhibit. She suggested the possibility of assembling similar floral exhibits for the railway, which she thought would be valuable in attracting tourists. The idea clicked, and, after leaving my boys, much to their delight, on a friend's farm at Thunder Bay, I was soon on my way leaving Yale, B.C., on a "speeder" of the type used by railroad maintenance crews, stopping an hour or so when and where we pleased. At such times the men lifted the motor off the main line as I pursued my mission.

I made no permanent stop until Sicamous, on the shores of Shuswap Lake, a clear mirror reflecting perfectly its lovely mountain setting. Here I gathered and mounted some of my most beautiful specimens, all found within four miles of the right-of-way. For the first time I saw the scarlet Indian paint-brush. (In Yukon this flower is either an ugly magenta or a sickly lemon colour. In fact, in all my Yukon rambles I have never found a really scarlet flower.) The hillsides were aglow with pink and blue or purple bearded tongue, while four-leaf clovers grew, not only singly, but in families and villages. Everywhere there was a riot of bloom, and I collected over 200 varieties.

In the vicinity of Sicamous, at Maro Lake, I came upon my most thrilling floral find, only a hundred feet from the railway. Walking aimlessly along the tracks one beautiful June morning, my eye caught a bright spot of yellow in the green marsh beyond. I scrambled across the ditch, through the underbrush, and into the bog. I was almost mired, but a few frantic struggles brought my reward. Spread before me, in a glory of golden colour and a profusion of bloom, was a wonderful natural bed of yellow orchids (*Cypripedium pubescens*) probably one that had never before been invaded by a flower seeker. There were hundreds of beautiful blossoms so superbly lovely that I looked at them a long time before I could bear to pick a single flower—to take one from its perfect surroundings. When I did, I smelled it, but there was practically no odour, although the hundreds of blossoms filled the air with an elusive fragrance as rare as it was enchanting.

At Sicamous, too, I found more beautiful butterflies and moths than anywhere. While I caught many by hard running, I discovered another way. I had noticed on warm drowsy days that butterflies hovered over moist places. I selected a place and poured over it an enticing concoction of syrup and Scotch whisky. Within a few hours a dozen or more gauzy beauties were helplessly intoxicated. Later, as I dropped them into the cyanide bottle prior to pressing them between the pages of a magazine, I had a few twinges of regret, but not enough to give them their freedom. After a severe rainstorm, on a tramp through the wet woods, I found many winged beauties hanging under leaves and branches.

From Sicamous I went to Glacier, where there was almost a complete change of flora. Here I found the saucy yellow violet; the dog-tooth violet or "glacier lily," as it is more appropriately called, a lemon-coloured flower growing over the mountainsides and in quantities at the foot of the Great and Asulkan glaciers, and higher up—after climbing over an exquisite carpet of pink-rose and white false heather—the dwarfed mountain larkspur and yellow columbine. Between Glacier and Golden were colourful patches of orange and scarlet lilies on the grey rocky mountainsides.

For a time I made my headquarters at Field, the little railway village under the frowning dome of Mount Stephen. As I wandered up and down the tracks I became acquainted with railway men and schedules of way freights. Whenever I wished to be picked up, I signalled them by placing in the middle of the track a piece of white cotton tied to a stick. At first the men were alarmed at my solitary trips, and warned me that I might meet tramps and hoboes. But I never met any dangerous individuals. I often shared my lunch with wanderers who seemed to be on the road for the sheer love of it. In this district were wonderful orchids—the rare white *Cypripedium passerinum*, coral root, lady's tresses, calypso, and fragrant white bog orchid.

From here I took the well-known Yoho valley trip, a jaunt of four days by horseback.

At noon the last day we came upon the Smithsonian Institution camp, in charge of Dr. A. Wolcott, the secretary, an authority on fossil vertebrates. He was superintending the digging of these fossils—this particular place being considered one of the greatest beds in the world. I was greatly concerned at the time that these should be taken from Canada, and wrote my opinion to Ottawa. I learned later that a division of his discoveries was ordered for the Ottawa museum. After lunch here we commenced the descent to Field, making the final stages as the clouds parted and the sun shone down on a glorious landscape.

I left Field and worked my way down to that world-famed beauty spot, Lake Louise, with its borders and terraces of brilliant-hued Arctic poppies, ranging from purest white to deepest orange, enhancing the grounds of a spacious mountain chalet. Here I noticed that pansies grew almost as large as in Yukon, while luscious wild strawberries were an unbelievable size.

It was but a step to "Banff the Beautiful," where I remained many weeks, the railway placing at my disposal spacious rooms in its fine hotel which commands a magnificent view of the Spray and Bow rivers. Father joined me here, and we had many delightful tramps far and wide over mountain paths. I recall being asked by the railway officials to look over and give suggestions for the de luxe camp being prepared for the Rothschilds, miles from any habitation, in the mountain fastnesses. It seemed to me to have every luxury—real beds, collapsible bathtubs, tables, chairs—all toted by pack ponies over seemingly impassable places.

I met many interesting people—Julia Hensaw, the well-known journalist and author of *Rocky Mountain Wild Flowers*; Mrs. Charles Shaffer, who illustrated Stewardson Brown's wild flower book; the Duke of Sutherland; Dr. and Mrs. Murphy, of Chicago, the former well known in the medical world as the inventor of the "Murphy Button," and the latter a St. Mary's graduate; Col. and Mrs. Longstaff and two sons; and the Westheads, he, Walter B., a well-known "City man" in London.

Summer waned, and with the first breath of fall the hardy golden rod, purple fleabane, and wild aster followed the golden gaillardia, harebells, orchids, and mountain lilies. Soon the mountainsides flamed with autumn foliage, and it was time to go home.

Who does not love flowers? And the mere gathering is the first step in a series of most fascinating nature studies. Mothers who are often at their wits' ends to keep children busy should send them picking flowers and show them how to press and mount them. Patience, fresh flowers, absorbent cotton, blotting paper, and cardboard are all that is needed. Here are the directions:

1. Place blotting-paper on cardboard and lay flowers between alternate layers of cotton and blotting-paper, taking care to tuck tiny wisps of cotton between each petal of many-petalled flowers.

2. Press under medium weight.

3. Open in 10 or 12 hours, to see if flowers are in good shape. If very moist, replace upper layer of cotton with fresh supply; press again lightly until dry.

4. When flowers are dry, remove all cotton threads with moist finger and thumb, using great care, as dried flowers are fragile and break easily.

5. When pressing lady's slippers, stuff pouch with tiny wad of cotton.

6. When preparing to mount flowers, sweep in background of suitable colouring on watercolour paper.

7. Study flowers with a view to using a wash that will best bring out the natural colours of the flowers.

8. Paste flowers on card with paste made from flour, to which may be added one-fifth mucilage and a liberal amount of salt.

9. Wash in shadows to make flowers stand out.

10. Cover with maline, pink, white, or yellow, and your "artistic flower" will be ready for the mat and frame.

11. In making score or place cards, maline is unnecessary, but narrow, bright-coloured ribbons add to the effect and general beauty.

Although this flower pleasure may be had at nearly every man's door for the taking, it is strange that to a "soulless corporation" (which we generally associate with hard-fisted money grabbers)—a great Canadian railway—goes the credit of the first organized effort to popularize this work—"artistic botany."

This is due in a large measure to Sir William Van Horne, whose policy of encouraging the arts has been continued by his successors in the presidency. I still have my letter of commendation from Sir Thomas Shaughnessy, who told me the only pictures in the royal suite at the Banff Springs hotel prepared for the visit of the Governor-General and his wife—the Duke and Duchess of Connaught—in July 1912, were those of my mounted wild flowers.

My summer's work brought an offer from the Belgian Government to do similar work for it. This would have meant spending three years in that country, and at the time I did not feel that I could break up my home and leave my growing boys, so, with reluctance, I declined the offer.

In 1924 and 1925 I prepared other exhibits for the Canadian Pacific Railway, which they sent to the Wembley Exhibition. ✸

Chapter XIV

CHATELAINE OF GOVERNMENT HOUSE

When I returned to Vancouver I found George in the throes of a Dominion election campaign—the famous Reciprocity election of 1911, when the Laurier Government went down to defeat on that issue. George himself was not running, but was in Yukon working night and day for the Conservative party in support of Dr. Alfred Thompson, and later stumping in Vancouver for Harry Stevens, later originator and only representative of the Reconstruction Party in the Canadian Parliament.

Echoes of the main issue of the campaign had reached me in Banff when Father was visiting me. He had received a letter from Uncle Charles Morse (Fairbanks Morse), saying:

> "There is an election campaign in Canada. The Government is advocating reciprocity between Canada and the United States. We have halted our building in Montreal and will do nothing in Toronto until after the election, for *if* reciprocity goes through it will not be necessary to build in Canada."

(Little did I think that this letter, a quarter of a century later, would become the governing factor in my decision to vote against the 1936 Reciprocity Bill in the Canadian House of Commons.)

The Conservatives carried the country, and next year George was appointed seventh Commissioner of the Yukon Territory.

Filled with joy at the opportunity to live again in the country we both loved so well, accompanied by Donald and Lyman, we left for the North in March. With nine or ten others, at Whitehorse we took the White Pass sleigh, to begin the longest continuous stage journey in the world (almost 400 miles). We jolted, slipped, and slid up and down steep and icy hillsides, over frozen rivers and lakes, stopping every 15 or 20 miles at roadhouses, where we changed horses, daily ate four $1.50 meals, and nightly rested in $2 bunks.

After journeying 10 days, eight miles from Dawson we were met by several sleigh loads of friends, and the reunion celebrated with suitable conviviality.

A few days later we were deeply touched by the huge official reception of the Territory, almost a thousand attending this event, which was held in the A.B. Hall in Dawson. "And they say Dawson is on the down grade . . ." I wrote in my journal.

We took up residence at once in Government House, which I soon found was conveniently laid out. On the first floor were the large drawing, reception, living, and dining rooms, kitchen, and pantry; the second, writing and bedrooms; the third, servants' quarters and billiard room. As no money had been allowed for renovation for years, the place was badly run down. Actually there were cracks in the kitchen and attic so large you could see outside. But I was soon heart and soul in the fixing of it.

As soon as we were settled I planned our first reception. My time had now come for the realization of a dream of years—that this beautiful "house of the people" should be open to all who wished to come, irrespective of social position.

Preparing for an indefinite number of guests with no precedent to guide me was an anxious bit of organizing, the only help from George being, "Madame, you run the house the way you like—but see that you have plenty to eat and drink."

We had a staff of servants—cook, butler, housemaid, gardener, and assistant. Much to the disapproval of our German cook and the ill-concealed amusement of the butler, I gave orders for 1,000 sandwiches, 40 cakes, 20 gallons of sherbet, and the same quantity of salad. Friends helped me make 20 pounds of home-made candy, and there were the makings of gallons of punch. I insisted that my orders be carried out to the letter, feeling that a failure to have enough to eat at my first reception would indeed be a calamity. My estimate of the appetites of my Yukon friends turned out to be accurate, for there was very little left over—only enough sherbet and salad for lunch the next day, half a fruit cake, and about a pound of candy. Fresh sandwiches and coffee had to be made for the select few who remained to talk the party over in the early morning hours.

The first guest arrived at 7:55 p.m., and from that time to 5 a.m. a steady stream kept coming and going. At midnight we had the rugs taken up so that we might dance, a five-piece orchestra having been engaged. Almost 600 attended. The highest compliment paid to its success was the remark of a well-known Tab, which was repeated to me: "The Blacks didn't have to go to Government House to learn how to entertain; they always did keep open house."

The following beautiful May days lured me out of doors, and I decided to concentrate on the garden, both for its use and beauty. I went into consultation with the "royal gardener," who also attended the furnace. (This latter was no small job either, as we burned wood to the cost of $2,200 each year). We decided to enlarge the greenhouse, add a root house, and raise our own vegetables. Our indefatigible work coupled with Arctic zone sunshine had extraordinary results.

We grew head lettuce, radishes, peas, carrots, beans, turnips, salsify, potatoes, celery, squash, and vegetable marrow. I sent outside for pounds of mushroom spawn, which was broken up and

YUKON ARCHIVES

Martha Louise on path behind Government House in Dawson, about 1915. St. Paul's Anglican Church stands in the background.

Mrs. Black, her buggy laden with flowers, makes a social call. As chatelaine of Government House, she enjoyed sharing the flowers from her garden.

Not content with her large garden, Martha Louise used the large windows of the Commissioner's residence to grow many plants indoors.

100

placed here and there in the garden and on the lawns. (Today quantities of mushrooms can still be found on the unoccupied grounds.) In the greenhouse we raised enormous tomatoes and cucumbers—the northern tomato being meatier than those grown outside. I cannot say that our gardening was economical, but it did make for good eating.

But I revelled in our flower gardens. We discovered that it was possible to winter out of doors many bulbs, corms, and roots, and we started many others in the greenhouse. We transplanted these, never later than 24th May, and soon the place was a riot of colour, with hundreds of daffodils, tulips, irises, jonquils, lilies of the valley, and even the old-fashioned bleeding heart. Our pansies were particularly lovely, these growing to abnormal size, many four inches across. As summer advanced we had every known variety of flower found in north temperate zone gardens. Against the house were canary creeper, trailing nasturtiums, delphiniums which came up yearly in a magnificent range of blue, pink, and mauve colourings, and snapdragons; along the fence sweet peas of every hue, and vines often growing to a height of 12 feet; behind the residence, on either side of the long path leading to the Commissioner's office, borders of California, shirley, and Oriental poppies in countless shades.

Having eaten cold storage food so many years in the North I decided to keep chickens to assure us a supply of fresh eggs and poultry. I sent to Vancouver for six dozen hens. They arrived and did their duty nobly—especially in the long-light summer days, but the long-dark winter days were not conducive to the laying of eggs. From a book, *Care of Chickens*, I read that a mixture of chopped meat and red pepper would remedy this, and I told the gardener to add this to the chicken feed.

We had at this time 30 laying hens, and within a few short days we seemed again to have plenty of fresh eggs. I began boasting about it—sending eggs to invalid friends. Every day the number increased. One day the cook reported 32 eggs! Thirty hens—thirty-two eggs! I went to the kitchen to investigate. Yes, there were plenty of eggs all right, but I discovered that George had been playing a joke on me. He had been buying eggs by the case. My boasted precious fresh eggs had been store eggs!

I was chatelaine of Government House four years, and we always kept open house. Everyone was welcome, but I did insist that there be no hoaxes. When a sourdough friend rang up saying, "May I come over tonight and bring the Missus," I replied, "You're sure she's your real wife. You have already introduced me to several 'wives,' and George and I owe a duty to the dignified office he holds."

Neither did I overlook the children's parties. Donald had graduated from high school, and was earning his way through Leland Stanford University, California, where he was taking engineering. Each summer holiday he came home, as he found it more advantageous to work for the Guggenheims than stay outside. But Lyman was with us all the time. I recall one Halloween party for him. I was determined to attack the problem of the usual rowdyism in which my boys played their part, by inviting a number of boys to Government House.

During the festivities I was startled by the ringing of the Anglican church bell. "For once they can't blame this on my children," thought I smugly. Citizens rushed to the church, but no traces of culprits could be found. Boasting of the boys' innocence at meal-time next day, I caught a wild gleam in Lyman's eye. "Lyman, you didn't . . . !"

"Surely, Mother, we didn't put that over you. We tied a rope from our upstairs window to the bell. We took turns ringing it. When you got excited one of the fellows cut the rope, slipped out, and took it off our lawn."

Lyman discovered a unique way of making pocket money. A former employee of the Bank of Commerce, which was next door to Government House, obtained a "lay" of the surface rights to the bank lot, and constructed a set of small sluice boxes into which he shovelled the surface dirt, washing it with water from the "borrowed" Government garden hose. He recovered several hundreds of dollars' worth of gold, mostly in the form of buttons from crucibles which had been handled by the bank. Later, when the building was moved, the carpenters, using the same equipment, washed up more gold from immediately under the bank floor. Then along came Lyman and his school chum, and again using the same sluice boxes and Government hose, sluiced an additional $75 worth of dust.

During George's term of office, among our distinguished guests were John F. Strong, Governor of Alaska, and his wife, a remarkably fine pianist, who visited us on a trip out; Sir Douglas and Lady Hazen, the former a member of a notable Loyalist New Brunswick family and Minister of Marine in the Borden Government. Preparations were under way for a visit from Their Royal Highnesses the Duke and Duchess of Connaught (the former Governor-General), but the war changed their plans.

Women's clubs began to penetrate into Yukon in 1912. While at Government House I organized the first chapter of the Imperial Order Daughters of the Empire (I.O.D.E.), this called the Dr. George M. Dawson Chapter, named after the leader of the government geological expedition sent out in 1887 to explore "that portion of the North-West Territories drained by the Yukon River." When organizing this chapter I well remember the impertinent remark of one young woman: "Many of us, Mrs. Black, are interested to know how long one has to be a Daughter of the American Revolution before becoming a Daughter of the Empire?" I smiled and replied, "Only until one marries George Black." I also organized a girls' chapter, named after one of our heroic police officers, Inspector Fitzgerald, who lost his life the year before when in charge of the Dawson-McPherson patrol.

One of the greatest traditions of the North West Mounted Police centres around Inspector Fitzgerald and the lost patrol of the winter of 1910-11. It was the time of the annual police trek along the rim of the Arctic from Fort McPherson to Dawson. With an ex-Mounted Policeman as a guide, Inspector Fitzgerald and two members of the force had started from McPherson in December and were due to arrive in Dawson by the end of January. They did not arrive. February drew to a close and still they had not come. Nor was there any word of them. The whole town became aroused. Anxiety grew so intense that a search patrol was ordered from Dawson. This was in charge of Sergeant Dempster, one of the most capable and fearless men of the force, who took with him three others of the police and an Indian guide.

From the window of Government House I watched the patrol set forth. Later Dempster described this trip to me. "Almost three weeks had gone by, when we discovered traces of white men's camps on the Little Wind River bank. We supposed them to be Fitzgerald's camp, and suspected that the patrol had been forced to turn back for lack of food, as there were evidences that the men who had camped there had killed and eaten their dogs. Within 25 miles of McPherson we came upon the frozen emaciated forms of two members of the party, huddled together under a pile of blankets. We now felt certain of the fate of the others. Eight miles farther on we found the lifeless forms of Inspector Fitzgerald and his companion, frozen beside a dead campfire, over which hung a pot of ice containing pieces of leather and moosehide, mute evidence of the tragic struggle to ward off starvation."

With Fitzgerald's body was his diary, the last entry being made on 5th February. It told how he had lost the trail at Little Wind River, and of 10 days' fighting through blizzards to find it; of the decision to turn back toward Fort McPherson as their rations were running low; of their sicknesses, especially scurvy, which they blamed upon eating dog's liver; of the agony of the final struggle.

In his pocket was this brief will:

"All money in despatch bag and bank, clothes, etc., I leave to my dearly beloved mother, Mrs. John Fitzgerald, Halifax. God bless all."

Life pursued the even tenor of its way until August 4, 1914. That memorable night George and I were entertaining a theatre party in Dawson's one moving picture house, which was crowded to the doors.

During an interval a telegram addressed to Hon. George Black, Commissioner of Yukon, was handed to my husband. He read it, and without comment passed it to me. "England is in a state of war with Germany," was the message from the Secretary of State at Ottawa.

The news was not entirely unexpected, as our daily paper had been featuring the European situation with huge headlines. Yet when the blow fell it was both startling and sudden. Immediately the Commissioner went to the stage, and raising his hand, in a voice filled with emotion, read the telegram. Men and women looked at each other in silence, aghast, trying to realize the significance of the words.

Twenty scarlet-coated members of the Royal North West Mounted Police were seated in the centre of the theatre. Two of these, brothers, former members of the Coldstream Guards, well over six feet in height, looked at each other and whispered to the other members. As though answering an overwhelming urge, they stood and in unison commenced to sing "God Save the King." The effect was electrical. With one move the audience was on its feet, and never in the world, I dare say, was our national anthem sung with greater fervour or more depth of feeling than in that moving picture house in that little town on the rim of the Arctic. Although 8,000 miles of mountain, land, and sea separated us from London, the heart of Empire, yet England's King was our King, and England's Empire was our Empire. We realized as never before that we were not English, nor Irish, nor Scotch, nor Welsh, nor yet Canadian, but *British*, bound together by the Anglo-Saxon ties of blood.

From then on life lost all serenity. There was no contented settled-down feeling. From week to week, month to month, men began leaving Yukon—not to the inspiring sounds of massed bands nor the thrilling sight of magnificent battalions marching past—no, only in response to a still small voice within, "Your King and Country need you!" With packs on their backs they mushed from 200 to 400 miles. I knew one man who walked 300 miles to enlist, and was rejected because of flat feet. Could a joke go further? (Both he and a brother finally got to France.)

Month by month I could see that George was growing more restless. I hurled myself into war work—Red Cross, I.O.D.E., and completed two St. John's Ambulance first-aid courses, to be ready for the time I knew was coming.

It came in the spring of 1916. I have it recorded in my journal:

"George has just come in and told me he has to enlist—that he cannot stand it any longer, seeing our men go away, while he sits in his office and we have the comfort of this beautiful home.

"Of course, there's nothing for me to do but to act as though I like it. It will be a wrench—to leave this lovely place. There's the dreadful anxiety of our future, too. What will this horrible war bring forth? I dare not think of it. Yet why should I hesitate or try to keep him back? Thousands, yes, millions, already have suffered the horrors of this terrible war for over a year."

George Black, seventh Commissioner of the Yukon, sent in his resignation to Ottawa, and organized a Yukon Infantry Company, of which he was appointed captain. This is his recruiting letter:

"Commissioner's Office,
"Dawson, Y.T., *August* 1916.

"Dear Sir,

"Men are needed to complete the Yukon Infantry Company for Overseas Service. You cannot fail to realize that it is the duty of every able-bodied man in Canada, who is not supporting helpless dependents, to offer his services to fight for the Empire in this great crisis.

"That Yukon has done well, that many of her Men have gone, that Yukon women are doing their duty, does not relieve you. It is a matter of individual manhood. Each must decide for himself whether or not he will play the part of a man.

"We have remained at home in safety while others have been fighting our battles for over two years, although no more obligated to do so than you or I have been. They have, for us, in many cases, made the supreme sacrifice. They are calling to you and to me for help. Are we going to fail them, or will you come with us?

"Yours very truly,
"George Black, *Captain,*
"Yukon Infantry Company, C.E.F."

He got a splendid response. I recall his telling me that he noted that one of his friends, an Englishman from "up the creek," was not speaking to him. He stopped him and said, "What's the matter with you?"

"Matter with me! You've asked every damned man in this town to enlist but me!"

"And who in hell got us into this war? Wasn't it the English? You ought to know enough to enlist." A grinning recruit signed up.

One of the first to join George's company was Lyman, who, like a dozen or more Yukon boys, was far too young to go. Warren wrote that he was to command a troopship moving Siamese troops. Donald was still at Stanford, within a few months of graduation, but was granted his degree on his school record and his purpose to enlist.

All my men in war service. What was there for me to do? There was only one answer. Follow them! ✵

Chapter XV

I GO TO LONDON

The Yukon Infantry Company, 275 strong, recruited and commanded by Captain George Black, left Dawson on the *SS Casca*, October 16, 1916. Aside from them and the ship's crew, I was the only other person aboard—and the only woman. For the time being my sadness and anxiety over leaving our beautiful home and many friends, and going we knew not where, were submerged in the comfort that I was with my husband and son.

The soldier boys had been given a rousing farewell banquet, with many speeches. They had been showered with gifts—tobacco and

George Black became officer commanding of the troopship SS Canada, *and Martha Louise was the only woman among 3,500 men aboard.*

candy (to last several months), socks, and other necessities. I do not remember the donors of these, but I do recall we were all deeply touched by the gift from the Japanese of Dawson—tobacco to the value of $69.

I had been feted and honoured to the degree of being ashamed to accept more attention. My dear friends had formed a "Martha Munger Black Chapter" of the I.O.D.E. Another group had collected a sum of money, the Yukon Comfort Fund, which they entrusted to me to be spent on the boys at my discretion.

The entire population seemed to be at the waterfront to see us off. The *Dawson News* was distributing souvenir numbers headlined with "FIGHTING MEN OF THE NORTHLAND SAY GOOD-BYE. EPOCH-MAKING OCCASION IN HISTORY OF YUKON."

The hoarse whistle of the boat signalled "All ashore." There were last hurried tearful farewells. As we drew away from the wharf, mid loud cheering, the band struck up "Tramp, Tramp, the Boys are Marching," and I recall the verve of the singing of this Yukon wartime parody:

> *"There's a land of pale blue snow,*
> *Where it's 99 below,*
> *And the polar bears are dancing on the plain;*
> *In the shadow of the Pole,*
> *Oh, my love, my own, my soul,*
> *I will meet you when the ice worms nest again.*

> *Chorus*
> *"Tramp, tramp, tramp, the boys are marching,*
> *Cheer up, Dawson, we'll return.*
> *When the Kaiser's on the blink,*
> *We'll sail back across the brink,*
> *And put the old town on the hum again.*

> *"There's a land of midnight sun,*
> *Where Boyle's dredges groan and hum,*
> *And the ptarmigan are warbling in the trees.*
> *And the whiskey that they sell*
> *Makes you wish you were in—well,*
> *Our thoughts will float to you on every breeze."*

We were like a big family party, and there were many surprises on the way out. The Martha Munger Black Chapter had made "housewives" (small sewing kits which the men called "hussies") on which were handworked names of each member of the company. They had also knitted several pairs of socks for George and each of the others. These were presented with due ceremony. I, too, was called forth to receive a poke of gold nuggets, one from each member of the chapter. I have these to this very day—my "ace in the hole" in the last round of this game of life.

The boys felt that these gifts merited a verse of thanks from the company's poet, Sergeant Barwell, with this result:

> *"Daughters of the Empire, please accept our hearty*
> *thanks*
> *For your thoughtfulness—you really have been kind;*
> *Though we're resolute and happy, yet the Captain and*
> *the ranks*
> *Still cast a longing lingering look behind.*

> *"We have stolen Mrs. Black, and we will not bring her*
> *back*
> *Till the Germans quit, and when the Allies win,*
> *Till we nail the Union Jack on the Kaiser's chimney*
> *stack,*
> *And we toast the Yukon daughters in Berlin."*

The Martha Munger Black Chapter had given me several yards of white linette to make an autographed quilt, which they intended to raffle to raise funds for war work. The men helped me tear this into four-inch squares, on which they autographed their names. These were sent back to be worked with red cotton. We bought and sold dozens of chances at two bits apiece. Months later I learned I was the lucky winner. I gave the quilt to Lyman as a wedding gift.

The company went in training at Victoria, British Columbia. Early in January George received orders to "Stand by."

I determined to try to go overseas on the troopship with him. To determine was easy, but to untangle the yards of official red tape which would permit a wife to go over on a troopship with her husband, this third year of the war, was another and no small matter. I decided to go to Ottawa and try to get permission.

While there I interviewed everybody who might have influence or authority in the matter—Sir Robert Borden, the Prime Minister, our old friend Sir Douglas Hazen, Minister of Marine. Lady Hazen helped me considerably by making several personal calls on my behalf. I found all "so sympathetic," but the only answer I received from the powers that be was that they would raise no objections if General Bigger, officer commanding transportation at Halifax, would consent.

I hurried to Halifax, saw the general, who was pleasant, smooth, but evasive.

"But, Mrs. Black, you wouldn't want to be the only woman on board a ship with 2,000 men, would you?" he asked.

"General Bigger, I walked over the Chilkoot Pass with thousands of men and not one wanted to elope with me."

"Well, we'll see, we'll see!" was the only satisfaction I got.

The Yukon Company arrived. George was to be officer commanding troops aboard ship the *SS Canada*. He went at once to General Bigger for orders, and Lyman went immediately with the others to the ship. I was left alone several long weary hours fairly "hanging by the gills." "Well, you can go," were George's first words when he returned. He also told me that General Bigger had called him aside, saying, "Your wife tells me you want her to go to England with you. I have held back permission until I found out from you personally if you really want her. Some husbands

The 275 men of the Yukon Infantry Company at Seaford, England, in March 1917. The X marks Captain George Black, who formed the company in Dawson.

prefer their wives to stay at home." (That's just one example of how men gang together.)

I was so thrilled that even now I find it difficult to express it. In my journal I have recorded:

> "I AM GOING. The ship leaves in an hour. There may be danger, but who cares? I can face anything with my loved ones at my side."

It was an eight-day voyage, and according to Captain Davies the stormiest trip he had experienced on the North Atlantic in five years. The vessel tumbled about like a cockle shell, and for several days we were lost to the other troopships and our convoy, the French destroyer *Admiral Aub*.

The press gave much publicity to the arrival of the Yukoners, "who had come 8,000 miles to fight for the Empire." They told how we had sent 10 per cent of our population to fight for King and Country; that we had given $20 a head to the patriotic fund—more than any other part of Canada. The members of the Boyle-Yukon Machine Gun Battery had distinguished themselves, all original officers getting military crosses, 24 men military medals, and 1 man a D.C.M. for conspicuous gallantry at Passchendaele.

We had cards of admission to the House of Commons. George was taken to the Distinguished Visitor's Gallery, while I was led by devious ways and dusty passages to the top of the building and put behind an iron grille in the Ladies' Gallery. I told some of the members later that this was my first visit to a country where men were so frightened of women that they had to keep them behind bars!

Everywhere I was introduced as "The Lady from the Yukon." "Is it cold there?" was always the question, and my invariable answer was, "I have never suffered with cold there as I have here." And it was true—the misery of trying to keep warm over grate fires which barely took the chill off the rooms! It was a criminal waste of fuel, too, as most of the heat went up the chimney. Our little Klondyke stoves could have warmed the rooms with half the fuel. Preparing for the night was a real ceremony. First I took a "red hot" bath, then put on my long-sleeved, high-necked flannel nightgown and bed-socks, and crawled into a bed warmed by two hot-water bottles. To think I had to go to London to get chilblains!

Occasionally someone would say, "Yukon, where is that?" One of our officers overheard that question, just before undergoing an operation. An attendant answered, "Oh, I don't know. Probably somewhere in China." The patient, whose previous lack of vitality had been causing considerable anxiety, raised himself and shouted, "Hell! Yukon is in Canada . . . near the North Pole!" The operation was successful.

As each visit from George and Lyman ended, we thought it might be the last before they were ordered to the front—yet we seldom spoke of it. Finally they did go, leaving me trying so hard to be brave, to cultivate the habit of believing all was well, to convince myself of the utter uselessness of worry, to prepare myself, even if the worst came, to take the blow.

At 19, Lyman Black was awarded the Military Cross at Buckingham Palace by King George V, while his proud mother looked on.

As I was the only Dawson woman in London, many of our boys made my small flat home when on leave. They took the place of my own boys and helped me forget my troubles, for there were times when I did not know where any of my sons were. They brought along their buddies to visit me. Both Canadians and Americans seemed so glad to meet anyone from the other side of the Atlantic. They told me their troubles and joys. Perhaps they hadn't received their letters from home (I didn't get mine either—probably lost at sea.) They showed me pictures of "my wife and kids" or "my girl." Sometimes they asked advice.

I was a very proud Yukon mother, too, when the press of the day was featuring "the bravery of a Yukon youth of 19, who caught a company of Hun cavalry as they rushed through a chance gap in our lines." That youth was my son Lyman. He was awarded the Military Cross.

The morning of the Investiture was a busy one at our little flat. The boy had his buttons and shoes to shine, his uniform to brush (no batman there), while I was excitedly getting breakfast and donning my very best dress.

We (relatives and close friends) had received beautifully engraved invitations, "with the compliments of the Master of the Household, Derek Keppel," to witness the Investitures, which were to be held in the grounds of Buckingham Palace—"weather permitting" outlined on the card in red ink.

On arrival at the palace, Lyman was ushered into the hall, while I was taken to the garden, where an inner quadrangle was roped off with thick scarlet woollen cords. The King and his aides, all in full service uniforms, arrived, followed by about 200 others, 20 of whom were nursing sisters. Although I had seen King George V many times, from my very good seat I had my first opportunity of watching a continuous performance in which he played a leading part. I thought him very attractive, especially when he smiled, more with his eyes than his mouth. He was just beginning to get grey, and looked very dignified and fine in his uniform, resplendent with red tabs and rows of decorations.

After Lyman received his decoration, "the M.C.," a handsome silver cross pendant from a crown, the whole hanging from blue and white moire ribbon, he went to an anteroom of the palace, where he was given a box for his cross, then outside to be photographed by the Canadian official photographer.　　　　➤✖◄

Chapter XVI
OVERSEAS SERVICE

I never worked as hard in my life as I did those overseas years. After three months of arduous steady service in the Prisoners-of-War Department, the routine became disorganized by loss of Canadian mails, delays of prisoners-of-war letters, governmental regulations cutting the amount of food parcels in half, an epidemic of measles (which meant double shift), and two personal attacks of appendicitis. I filled in the odd hours by doing Y.M.C.A. canteen work, attending meetings and investigations of the Women's Battersea Pension Board, sewing for the Red Cross, administering the Yukon Comfort Fund, visiting wounded Yukoners in hospitals, giving lectures on "The Romance of the Klondyke Gold Fields," writing letters to family and friends and to two Yukon papers, as I was "our own correspondent" for the *Dawson News* and *Whitehorse Star*. I tried magazine writing, but when I came to the actual recording, my pen scratched, my typewriter needed cleaning, and when this was done, inspiration was ever jeering at me from the bough of some distant tree outside my window, and I set to work darning socks.

People used to envy my opportunity for service, but there were many times I was deeply discouraged. My poor efforts seemed like those of a caged squirrel, always turning the wheel but to no avail. Like so many others not in front line service I felt indeed only on the outside looking in.

I shall never forget the week of anguish when Lyman was reported missing and the great joy when he was located. I would go in rags the rest of my life if we all could be in our Yukon home again, I thought. Would those days ever return; days of peace and prosperity, and would we ever renew old friendships or become the happy care-free people of olden days?

Warren had been ordered to Bangkok, Siam, to bring an interned German ship to San Francisco, I did not know where Donald was, and I received word of Father's death.

The air raids more than anything else brought personal realization of the horrors of war, and I went through 12. It is a fearful and nerve-racking sensation to know that sudden death is lurking in the heavens above you.

Whenever I was in the depths of discouragement, Battersea was the place to go to. There wives and mothers of disabled soldiers living on mere pittances, and bringing up families, were so uncomplaining and cheerful. This work took one very full day a week, when I left my flat at 8 a.m. and was seldom home before 7 p.m. My job was taking down statements of applicants for pensions, with pursuant investigations.

The Yukon Comfort Fund buying meant hours of shopping in crowded stores. After the battery went up the line the casualties were heavy, and some days I'd visit as many as seven of our boys in hospital, always taking some "comfort."

The boys were so appreciative of these visits and gifts that at Christmas 1917 the Yukon Machine Gun Battery presented me with their badge—specially made in gold.

I particularly enjoyed talking about my Yukon, on which I gave almost 400 lectures—the majority illustrated. I averaged a daily talk for months, to audiences which numbered 50 to 700. One day I gave three, but this was too much.

My most strenuous lecture trip was one lasting three weeks under the auspices of the Y.M.C.A., in South Wales, where the barren rugged Cambrians reminded me of the hills of home which flank the Yukon and Klondyke rivers. It meant catching trains at all hours to all places, carrying heavy boxes of slides and clothes, blocks on end in all kinds of weather, and all kinds of accommodation, from the humblest to the highest, as my hospitality was provided.

Once I spoke at Church House, London, on the "Missionaries of Yukon," having been invited to take the place of His Lordship Bishop Stringer of our Territory. On arrival I was shown into a committee room with 15 clergymen, bishops and others, who eyed me with as much suspicion as though I were a bomb. After we had waited 10 minutes, the Bishop of London arrived, breathless and apologetic for being late—he had been visiting troops with the King. We hurried to the platform, where his Lordship made a few preliminary remarks, mentioning all speakers but me. When he introduced me, in my turn on the programme, he said, "Oh yes,

Mrs. George Black, wife of the Commissioner of Yukon, will speak. I think she is what they call a 'sourdough.' " (Later I was asked if they called me this because I made sour bread.)

By this time I was provoked at his casual treatment as I has been officially invited to speak. I began, "My Lord Chairman, my lords, ladies, and gentlemen, if this be the way you usually treat women who are invited to address you I do not wonder suffragettes go around with axes over here."

The Bishop half arose, began to speak, but I continued, "My Lord, several times in London I have had to listen to you without interrupting when I should have very much liked to do so. Now please listen to me without interruption." The audience of some 500 applauded. I then expounded the theory of my basis of married life (harmony in religion, politics, and country), and continued: "And so, because I married an Anglican, I am one. But had I married a Fiji Islander I would probably be eating missionary now instead of talking missionary."

After tea a meek little "picked-sparrow" type of woman said to me, "You do not really mean that you could eat missionaries, do you?" The Bishop of London was with the group, and, looking at

The Boyle Yukon Motor Machine Gun Battery, organized and financed by the Blacks' old friend Joe Boyle. Gold from his own dredges adorns their uniforms.

him, I said, "Well—I did feel like taking a bite out of His Lordship." He laughed heartily at this.

My lecture work resulted in a distinctive honour. On July 18, 1917, I was elected a Fellow of the Royal Geographical Society. My name was proposed by Miss Pullen-Bury, F.R.G.S., F.R.A.I., author of *From Halifax to Vancouver*, and seconded by Sir Thomas Mackenzie, High Commissioner for New Zealand.

One quiet Sunday afternoon in the spring of 1918 I was busy preparing a chicken dinner for several Yukoners who were on leave, and who had given me their food coupons for this spread. The doorbell rang, and on answering it I was delighted to see my old Klondyke friend, Joe Boyle. I knew our boys would give no other man in the world a greater welcome than our own Joe Boyle, who at the time was being heralded everywhere as the "Saviour of Roumania."

Ten days after war was declared he had offered to equip a contingent of 50 Yukoners, to be known as the Boyle Yukon Motor Machine Gun Battery. With almost uncanny foresight, this great adventurer recognized the part motor machine guns were to take in the war. The offer was accepted, and in October 1914, 50 of our men left Dawson.

But my friendship with Joe Boyle, who might have been the hero of a dozen Henty books, began in the gold rush days of the Klondyke, when my brother George was managing Joe's laundry. Joe was then a young man—the roving son of one of Ontario's well-known stock breeders. Brought up in the quiet seclusion of an eastern farm, he filled his mind and heart with stories of the sea, and before his eighteenth birthday had run away from home and was sailing before the mast. Adventure met this Canadian boy at every turn.

Back in Canada, he became interested in trotting horses, this taking him to the racetrack centres of the States. Then came news of the Klondyke gold strike. Among the many excited thousands who met the northern ships at Seattle in 1897 with their "tons of gold" was Joe Boyle. He formed a partnership with Frank Slavin of prize ring fame, and they got as far as Skagway. They had no money to go on to Dawson. Joe could play the banjo and sing popular songs to his own accompaniments, so he and Slavin formed a vaudeville team and sang and boxed their way to Dawson. Here they started a steam laundry, made money, and Joe sold out.

Again he hit the trail, to ask from the Canadian Government a concession of mining land. He saw the possibilities of hydraulicking and dredging the valley of the Klondyke River. He succeeded in interesting influential men in his mission, and returned to Dawson with a concession of 40 square miles of mining leases. The wealth of Golconda was his. He married and appeared to have settled down for the rest of his life.

During these years he contributed much to the life of Dawson. A man of iron build, good-looking, a dominant personality, he was welcomed everywhere. 'Tis true he was quarrelsome, overbearing, and intolerant, determined to the point of obstinacy in business dealings, but we who knew him intimately and treasured his friendship found him gentle and kind, at times generous to a fault, and possessed of a great love for children, animals, and poetry. Most of all he was loved by the children of Dawson. Every year he gave them a picnic, at which he romped and played with them, seemingly enjoying it as much as they did.

Then came the declaration of war! Although he had organized and personally financed the first Yukon contingent, he had been left behind. Gold, gold, and more gold, was needed for the war. English stockholders clamoured for better returns, giant dredges wallowed deeper into the pay dirt, and the fires of the assayers burned hotter and brighter. But the heart of Joe Boyle beat in unison with the tramp of many feet thousands of miles across the sea.

The call of adventure and patriotism finally triumphed. The mines were left in charge of capable men, and Joy Boyle was soon in London, keen for action. He quickly discovered that he, to whom government red tape and diplomacy meant nothing, was only a small cog in the millions of wheels of the monstrous machine of war. He stamped and chafed at delay, but Joe Boyle was never known to give up. His persistence was of the constant-dropping sort that wears away a stone. Within a year he was sent to Russia in charge of British transportation in the Moscow area. Then came the Revolution, and he was ordered to take back Roumania's national treasure to Jassy from Moscow, where it had been sent for safe keeping.

During the days when Roumania was cut off from the Allies, surrounded by foes on all sides, her main road for transportation of food supplies completely blocked by the Bolsheviks, Boyle made many air flights to Odessa for provisions. He was placed in full charge of the Bessarabian railways. Undoubtedly but for him Roumania would have starved, and his deeds were considered by both the Roumanian and British governments as miraculous. He became a close personal friend of King Ferdinand and Queen Marie, who honoured him with many decorations. He came and went at will in the royal household, and the royal children called him "Uncle Joe."

Was it any wonder that I welcomed my old friend literally and figuratively with open arms that Sunday afternoon? As simply as one would tell of quiet days at home, he told me of his Russian and Roumanian experiences.

At this point the Yukon soldier boys arrived. The feast was spread and the Boyle stories told again, after which each man had tales of France, Belgium, or the Nile, and the wee sma' hours were upon us before good-nights were said.

Shortly after this Queen Marie was in London. She expressed a wish to thank Canadians personally for what Canada had done for Roumania, and so Sir George and Lady Perley (Sir George was then High Commissioner for Canada), invited about a hundred of us to be presented to Her Majesty.

George and I went with Joe Boyle, as we continued to call him. (A high official at Buckingham Palace, once said to me reproachfully, "You know, Mrs. Black, we always speak of him as Colonel Boyle," to which I replied, "He would be surprised and hurt if we ever called him anything but Joe.")

The room was well filled when the Queen entered, exactly to the minute. (I have discovered that royalty is always on time.) Sir Charles Cust, Sir George and Lady Perley, Lady Drummond, Lady Turner, and Matron Macdonald of the Canadian Nursing Service hastened to receive her, and a general tour of the room was begun.

Almost half the company had been presented when Queen Marie caught sight of Joe Boyle. At once she walked across the room, caught his hand and said, "Where have you been? We have not seen you for three days."

"I'm sorry, Your Majesty, I've been with old Yukon friends. I have two with me—Captain and Mrs. George Black. You've heard me speak of them often. Your Majesty, I should like to present them."

The Queen impulsively took my hand in both of hers, saying, "Then you know Colonel Boyle! He is a miracle man. He is

Roumania's Saviour. When everyone else ran away, deserted us, Colonel Boyle knew no fear. He remained. He saved our people."

By this time all eyes in the room were riveted on us. Time was passing; royalty has no spare moments, and others were waiting eagerly to be presented to the beautiful Queen. Smilingly she left us, saying, "Colonel Boyle will bring you to me again."

Later, when I was presented at the Roumanian Legation, I could not help noticing how dear "Our Joe" was to this lovely Queen and her family. She told me of the night of anguish when she and the King were saying good-bye to representatives of the Allies, who had been ordered back to their respective countries because of a forced armistice with Germany.

"Then came Joe Boyle. His very presence was a tower of strength. 'They have all gone,' I mourned. 'But I shall not leave,' was his reply. And Joe Boyle alone remained to console, help, and encourage." As she related this so feelingly, I noted she was wearing Joe's gift—his golden nuggets—with her glorious pearls.

While in England, Joe Boyle was paid much attention by all members of the royal family. However, no adulation turned his head, and he was always loyal to his old friends.

After the Armistice Joe became interested in Roumania's oil wells, which the exigencies of war had compelled the authorities to wreck. He again settled down to civilian work, but two attacks of paralysis sapped his strength and brought on a lingering illness. Cared for by a former Klondyke friend, Braden Burg, he died in England, April 24, 1923, and is buried in an old country churchyard.   ❧

Chapter XVII
THE ARMISTICE IS SIGNED

In the summer of '18 we who were close to the war picture knew of the plans for the big drive—and living became more intense. George wrote:

> " . . . We're down for the big move. No bomb proof jobs this time, but the boys are anxious to get going. We all feel we have horseshoes tied to us, and intend to play our luck. It has worked well to date. All leaves cancelled. . . ."

Then the blow fell. On 13th August I received one of those dreaded telegrams:

> "Sincerely regret to inform you Captain George Black, Infantry, officially reported admitted to Stationary Hospital, Abbeville, 11th August—gunshot wound—thigh."

Close upon this came a letter from George making light of his injuries, which he described as a "slam in the left leg with a chunk of shrapnel . . . and the right leg punctured with a machine-gun bullet."

> "I am lucky," he continued, "for this is as comfortable a 'blighty' as one could wish—a regular hand-picked one. If the hospital in France hadn't been so crowded they'd have patched me up over there, but by the second day of the big offensive there was standing room only, and the standing wasn't very good."

In a few days an orderly brought me a message from my husband. He had arrived at the Royal Free Hospital, London, and I could see him at once. In several weeks he was sent to the Convalescent Home at Matlock Baths, Derbyshire, and by October could get around fairly well.

Several weeks ahead we knew the war was ending. Hourly we awaited the signing of the Armistice. I can never forget that memorable morning of November 11, 1918, in London when it finally came.

George was now completely well and was ordered to the Rhine with the Army of Occupation. Lyman was with Colonel Muerling, O. C. Yukon Machine Gun Battery, who wrote me:

> "It may interest you to know that I have given Lyman command of the armoured cars in the official entry into Mons. I thought it might be of interest to Yukon to have the youngest member take part in such an historical event."

Next spring I was sent to France by the Overseas Club to visit soldiers' cemeteries and war-stricken villages with a view to observe rehabilitation and beautification schemes. Throughout that trip we saw the complete destruction and desolation caused by the war. We walked through street after street of deserted shelled houses with gaping windows, occasionally covered with flapping canvas. We trudged miles over battlefields, stumbling over rusty strands of barbed wire and almost falling into water-filled dug-outs and trenches.

And as far as the eye could see, symbolizing to me the tricolour of France, were patches of scarlet poppies and blue cornflowers against the dead white of the upturned chalk.

This spring of 1919 marked a highlight in my writing experiences, in that I was actually admitted to the British House of Commons, on a press ticket, representing my home papers, to hear Prime Minister Lloyd George declare his attitude on his pre-election promises concerning the peace treaty. My seat was directly behind that of the then Prince of Wales, who was seated "just over the clock." I watched him wriggle in his seat, fuss with his sword, and stroke an imaginary moustache. The Prime Minister talked two hours—but it seemed like 20 minutes. He explained the difficulties which beset the peace conference—the mighty questions of boundaries, indemnities, and punishments. His speech was replete with delicate satire, stinging sarcasm, sledgehammer blows of contempt for those who dared to try to cause trouble between the Allies, "whose friendship is essential to the peace and happiness of the world." If tense listening, followed by prolonged cheers from both sides of the House, were any criterion, Lloyd George had convinced the "Mother of Parliaments" that every pledge Britain had made would be incorporated in the demands of the Allies.

After returning from the war zone, I represented Yukon at a garden party given by Their Majesties King George and Queen Mary at Buckingham Palace, to which several thousand war workers were honoured with invitations. It was a beautiful day, and the flower-bordered lawns of the palace were enchanting in their summer beauty and fragrance.

We stood on either side of a long garden path. King George, Queen Mary, very beautiful in an embroidered dress and hat of her favourite blue, with a necklet of perfect pearls, and Princess Mary, smart in a V.A.D. uniform, walked between the lines. Now and again they stopped to speak to people they knew or to have others presented. When my turn came His Majesty asked several questions concerning my lecture work.

* * *

My overseas work was done. George had completed his Army of Occupation duties. The office of Commissioner or "Governor" of Yukon, which he had given up to enlist, had been merged with that of Gold Commissioner; the Yukon Council reduced to three councillors (elected from the districts of Dawson, Whitehorse, and Mayo); beautiful Government House had been closed, and to this day, except for the visit of Lord and Lady Byng, when the former was Governor-General of Canada in 1927, has not been reopened.

There was no position awaiting us in our own country. However, we decided to return to Canada, and although past the half-century mark, tired and childless (Lyman had decided to remain in military service), to try to reestablish ourselves.

I shall always be glad that I went overseas with my men. Talking over our small part in the Great War, we have all agreed many times that we had done the right thing, that if we had to make this decision again it would be the same. ➤✄◄

Chapter XVIII
WIFE OF THE FIRST COMMONER

O nce again George took up his law profession, opening an office in Vancouver. We bought a small cottage on the picturesque north shore of Burrard Inlet. In the soft sea-level air and beautiful environment my tired nerves relaxed, and I was soon restored to normal vitality, which for me always means an urge to be up and doing. I turned at once to gardening, for one has only to put a seed, slip, or root in the fertile land about Vancouver to have it grow. I became so fascinated that often I arose at 5 a.m. on glorious summer mornings to work in my pleasure-ground, sometimes pausing to watch the graceful ships in- and out-bound on the blue Pacific. On warm days, dressed in my bathing suit, I raked seaweed on the beach, as seaweed makes one of the finest fertilizers. Truly my garden was a "lovesome thing."

I was asked to speak at many meetings—to tell my war experiences, describe the wild flowers of British Columbia, or give illustrated Yukon talks. Whenever I feel my egotism swelling, and that people are clamouring to hear me speak, I remember the woman who, missing my meeting, said, "I did so want to hear Mrs. Black. I hear she's had her face lifted."

Speaking of demands on public women, I think some women's organizations might be more thoughtful in the treatment of guest speakers. They should at least provide hospitality, transportation, and incidental expenses.

We had been living in Vancouver two years when the federal election of 1921 was announced. Suddenly, like that well-known bolt from the blue, members of our political party waited on George to offer him the Yukon nomination. "You're the only man who can win the seat for the party . . . your overseas services . . . your previous record." He accepted, went north, and alone fought the hardest political battle of his life. He snowshoed up the Stewart River, 130 miles, to Mayo. When returning he had a miraculous escape from death in a motor accident—but broke three ribs. It

Martha Louise Black, wife of the First Commoner, in 1932.

125

was conceded generally that he had retrieved this seat for the Conservatives.

That winter we went to Ottawa, and from then on I have lived in Ottawa while Parliament is in session, Dawson in summer, and the remaining time en route between the two cities.

I recall one glorious winter trip out, in answer to a telegram, "Vitally important you be in Ottawa December tenth." This meant hurriedly closing our house and making a 4,000-mile journey by stage, boat, and rail to Ottawa. The boat was due to leave Skagway in eight days.

At 11 o'clock next night a jolly crowd of friends saw us off. We headed south in a Model T open touring car, to overtake at Hollenback's Roadhouse (20 miles beyond) the horse-drawn stage which

Headed south in a Model T open touring car on the first leg of a journey to Ottawa. The 4,000-mile trip continued by horse-drawn stage, boat, and rail.

had left that morning. It was a clear, cold aurora night, with gorgeous prism-coloured northern lights flaming and dancing across the heavens. We sped along in the bracing air, arriving at our destination at 3 a.m., whence, after a few hours' rest, we left on the stage next morning at seven.

On we went for miles, over a trail slashed out the fall before, the sleigh lurching and twisting on the rough road, stopping only to eat and to change horses. We were tired, sleepy, and low in spirits when we reached the large one-room log roadhouse where we were to spend the night. But dinner was ready, and such a dinner! Creamy barley soup, tender delicious moose steak and roast wild ducks, native cranberry jelly, celery, and head lettuce (grown in the garden and stored in the cellar), biscuits and cheese. Over coffee and cigarettes we discussed the news in month-old papers, and then retired to the comfortable, immaculately clean bed in a partitioned corner. As we left my host gave me a parcel—a ruffed grouse, plucked and stuffed, ready for the oven at the next road-house, where, as we rested, it was cooked and eaten.

Arriving at Stewart Flats, we met our old friend Joe Goulet, who was to drive us to Pelly Crossing. The Stewart River was not yet safe for a stage load, so we walked across, going the last 30 feet of that thin ice on duck boards. The horses were led singly, and the mail, our bags, express, were toted on hand-sleds—our crossing punctuated by occasional alarming cracks.

We arrived at the comparatively palatial two-storey log road-house at Stewart, and we fell to our evening meal with great gusto, the *piece de resistance* being caribou stew with dumplings.

The remainder of the journey was uneventful. We caught the *Princess Louise* at Skagway, and at Vancouver boarded the Canadian Pacific for Ottawa.

Telling of my trips in and out reminds me what airplanes have meant to the North, for none but a Northerner can appreciate their saving of time to travellers. Today I can come by plane from Dawson to Skagway in four hours, as compared with five days by boat and train, or five or six weeks when we mushed over the trail of '98. Every summer I do much of my visiting to constituents by plane.

But even more important is their significance in prospecting. Both Yukon and Alaska are vitally interested in each new mineral discovery, which, like the circle of a stone thrown into a pool, ever widens until the final ripple encompasses the whole, affects the livelihood of every man, woman, and child there.

To the foresight of Herbert Wheeler, pioneer railway man and general manager of the White Pass Route, and Livingston Wernecke, manager of the Treadwell Yukon Company, in large measure should go the credit of the introduction of the airplane in Yukon. Other names who have made air history are Everett Wasson, the first pilot, capable and courageous, and Joe Walsh, veteran prospector.

It is not surprising that Livingston Wernecke, when establishing aerial prospecting, should choose Joe Walsh, who had been successfully prospecting on the rim of the Arctic Circle for 20 years, a sure shot, good trapper, and most companionable.

It was my good fortune to be at the Wernecke camp, on the shores of Mayo lake, one perfect summer day, when the plane *Claire* took off on the first prospecting trip. An Indian had come in with the usual tale of a rich find. Mr. Wernecke decided it was worth investigating. He, Wasson, Walsh, and the Indian formed the first party. I well remember the men loading the supplies, which were taken to the plane by canoe. Walsh thought flour, bacon, tea, sugar, beans, salt, and dried fruits enough, but several luxuries were added. (Today, even for an hour's trip, compulsory supplies are bacon, hard tack, tea, matches, a gun, ammunition, and an axe.)

Finally all was in readiness. The plane taxied down the lake—one mile, two miles, five miles, then out of sight. In a short time it returned, as, after several futile attempts, it was found impossible to lift the heavy load. The canoe went out and some of the unessentials were unloaded. Again the plane took off. It sped down the lake, then arose gracefully from the water, circled over the hills in the distance, turned, and disappeared through the blue empyrean in search of the hoped-for El Dorado.

Wasson and Walsh were picked by Wernecke for an epic flight in search of the lost Burke party, who, prospecting for gold, had gone by plane too far into the hinterlands. Walsh, the old experienced prospector, and Wasson, the young efficient aviator, made a combination hard to beat. Each was willing to take the necessary chances, each fearless and tireless, each fully aware of the perils of the wilderness over which they flew, and each realizing that strength and supplies must be conserved.

They spoke of that flight (if they mentioned it at all) quite casually; that their search lasted three weeks; that they located the Burke camp, only to lose it again; that they finally walked 15 miles before they found it; that there were two survivors and one dead; that they helped the survivors to their plane, practically carrying them the last two miles.

This is the way with the men of the North—no heroics. So many have ploughed their weary ways through snowdrifts waist-high; climbed mountains; fought scurvy; carried sick comrades through miles of wilderness to help in far-flung settlements. So many have counted no task too difficult, but have met each day with the same fortitude which has inspired pioneers and pathfinders from time immemorial. Someone has said, "We have so many uncommon men in the North that they become common, just as in heaven angels are nobodies."

My husband won four successive federal elections— 1921, 1925, 1926, and 1930. At the earliest possible date after his first election he proposed and was successful in carrying through the Canadian House of Commons an amendment to the Yukon Act, which gave Yukoners the same rights to jury trial and in civil actions as people in other parts of Canada. He also drafted and sponsored the Yukon Quartz Mining Act, which placed lode and placer mining on the same basis. (The silver camp at Mayo had just been established.) This act made titles to mining properties secure and no longer subject to change by Orders-in-Council at Ottawa. In the following years he advised the Liberal Government of the day on a system of fair taxation on lode mining profits, and prepared a schedule whereby they returned substantial Government revenue without injury to the mining industry.

Bench by bench he was moved forward, and in 1930 was elected Speaker of the House of Commons, which made him "First Commoner," a position steeped in tradition. Not only does the Speaker preside over parliamentary sessions, but he is also official host of the House of Commons. When his name was proposed, the Rt. Hon. W. L. Mackenzie King, then leader of the Opposition, said he had no objection to the appointment, and wished to join the Prime Minister, the Rt. Hon. R. B. Bennett, in an expression of appreciation of George's qualifications, but he counselled him to leave partisanship behind—that, above all, the position needed the quality of impartiality—and then wished him well.

Mr. and Mrs. George Black on board ship to Ottawa after the 1930 election.

130

From my seat on the floor of the Senate Chamber I watched the opening of this seventeenth Parliament of Canada since Confederation. I heard the boom of the guns which heralded the arrival of His Excellency the Governor-General Lord Willingdon, and Her Excellency Lady Willingdon, with their party and cavalry escort. We stood as the vice-regal party entered the Red Chamber, and His Majesty's representative took his seat on the dais under the red canopy. Following him, Her Excellency, looking very queenly, wearing a coronet of diamonds and a handsome black gown, with court train, silver-embroidered in Greek-key pattern, borne by two pages, took her seat to the left. I see again the Prime Minister, Mr. Bennett, to the right, in Windsor uniform of gold-braided coat, white satin breeches, buckled shoes, and long stockings; the brilliantly coloured uniforms of military officers; the red woolsack, on which sat the Chief Justice and Supreme Court judges in their scarlet and ermine robes and cocked hats; the Sergeant-at-Arms carrying the mace, the massive gold staff surmounted by the crown; the Gentleman Usher of the Black Rod, and His Excellency, bowing in formal procedure; the diplomatic corps, representing many nations; the galaxy of beautiful women in gorgeous gowns contrasting with the formal black and white of the senators and unders.

The Gentleman Usher of the Black Rod was dispatched to the House of Commons with the message that His Majesty's Representative would receive his loyal Commoners to hear the speech from the throne. They came noisily to the bar of the Senate Chamber. Later I remarked to my husband how very rude it was that these members kept up a chattering during the reading of this speech. "You forget that we are the Commons, and this is in accordance with a tradition affirming our importance," he explained. He also told me that to assert further their importance, when they trooped back to their chamber, before dealing with the speech from the throne, a private member always brought in an innocuous resolution, which was never considered again during the session.

Usually, after the opening ceremonies, the House rises, but this was an emergency session, called immediately after the election to consider the unemployment problem, as it was the beginning of the depression. The House of Commons sat at once to deal with the speech from the throne.

That evening we entertained at a large dinner-party at the Chateau Laurier, and I remember the predominating colour of the women's gowns was "Tory blue."

When Parliament was in session I attended the sittings regularly, and always found the debates interesting and instructive. I still think the members speak too long, although I realize that they are speaking to their constituents through Hansard.

As wife of the First Commoner I was official hostess at a reception in the Speaker's Chambers immediately after the opening of Parliament. In addition to receiving, my duty was to choose refreshments and decorations. In this I owe a debt of gratitude to Ruggles (that is his real name) and Lavesque, who know so well how to manage state affairs. Ruggles had been brought to Canada by the Willingdons, whom he had served 25 years. When they left he wished to remain, and Lord Willingdon asked the Speaker to keep him on. Lavesque has been in the parliamentary restaurant for years. It was always a pleasure to plan these functions, which were usually attended by 800 to 1,200. There was every facility to carry them out—the finest of linens, the most beautiful china, silver, and cut glass, quantities of exquisite flowers, and perfect service.

The three most memorable affairs at which I was hostess during my husband's term as Speaker were the dinner which Their Excellencies Lord and Lady Bessborough honoured us by attending; a men's luncheon to honour Lord Byng; and a dinner complimenting Miss Mildred Bennett, sister of the Prime Minister, and Major W. D. Herridge, K.C., D.S.O., prior to their marriage.

Other functions of national importance come to me: a reception in honour of Their Imperial Highnesses Prince and Princess Takamatsu of Japan, at which the Speaker of the Senate and Madame Blondin, and the Speaker of the House of Commons and I received on behalf of the Government of Canada. George presented Her Royal Highness with a magnificent bouquet of scarlet carnations and calla lillies—chosen because they were of the Japanese royal colours. As the Prince and Princess left Parliament Hill they commented on the size, splendour, and magnificence of the buildings and the lovely view from the Peace Tower.

Sometimes we were called upon suddenly to arrange official social affairs for diplomatic and other prominent visitors. One night, after the House of Commons had adjourned (11 p.m.),

George telephoned that the Prime Minister had asked him if I would arrange a luncheon in honour of the Spanish Ambassador to the United States, Signor Carderas, and his wife, who were accompanying Mrs. Herridge (later the wife of the Canadian Minister at Washington) to the Capital next day. We worked on the guest list until 2 a.m., and the invitations were delivered by messenger before noon next day. A note in my diary says that all went smoothly and the luncheon was a success.

Another occasion was the visit of Col. and Mrs. Charles Lindbergh and Miss Morrow, who, with Col. MacNider (United States Minister to Canada) and Mrs. MacNider, occupied seats in the Speaker's Gallery in the House of Commons at one of the sessions. Later the party had tea with us in the Speaker's Chambers. We both enjoyed meeting the famous flier and his wife, whom we found pleasant and unassuming young people.

Living in the Capital, I soon learned that Ottawa society was divided into several sets—the Government set, changing with every election; the permanent Government staffs; and the representatives of foreign countries, whose duty it is to attend all formal state functions and "more or less" put in an appearance at informal affairs.

Members of the two old-line parties come and go, usually with no delusions of being able to carry through personal ideas of saving the country. I have watched the arrival of the Progressives, the Canadian Commonwealth Federationists and now the Social Credit members, all enthused with their socialistic ideas to pass legislation that would place all the people on an equal basis of living, or make the State guarantee a monthly income. I have seen their zeal for reform rise and fall, and my observation is that the old saying, "Rome was not built in a day," still holds. However, I do think we have speeded up the pace of reform legislation, and are more alive to the people's needs of rapidly changing times. Laws made today are revolutionary as compared with those of 50 years ago.

After the Imperial Conference George and I sailed for Europe on a holiday. He was hailed everywhere as "Member for the North Pole" as well as Speaker of the Canadian House of Commons. We were entertained widely—tea at No. 10 Downing Street with Premier and Mrs. Stanley Baldwin; dinner at which the Hon. Howard Ferguson, High Commissioner for Canada, and his attractive wife, Mrs. Ferguson, were host and hostess; and were

George Black as Speaker of the House of Commons.

honoured by an invitation to have high tea with Her Royal Highness the Princess Louise. She knew Robert Service well and asked if there really had been such persons as Dangerous Dan McGrew or Sam McGee. . . .

I was received by Her Royal Highness the Duchess of York, who looked charmingly pretty in a simple rose-red frock, with no ornaments save a string of pearls. She asked many questions of distant Yukon. She said she was sorry that the Princess Elizabeth (now Queen) was not at home, that she had gone for a skating lesson, and she herself had promised to go later and see what progress she was making, but would I like to see Princess Margaret Rose? Of course I would, and the bright-eyed, fair-haired little girl, about three years old, came tittuping into the room. Her mother introduced me. "How do you do, Mrs. Black?" and "Good-bye, Mrs. Black," were the only words she said to me. Then she was off to play in the garden, but she didn't want to put on her rubbers. . . . Her mother said she must put on her rubbers. . . .

Her Royal Highness told me of an occasion when her husband, the future King George VI, "kept an eye on" Princess Margaret Rose for an hour. Like many fathers on similar occasions, he was soon deeply engrossed in a magazine. In the meantime the butler laid the tea-table. Somehow the deep silence of the room caused him to raise his eyes from his magazine, and there was little Margaret Rose with two small fists into the middle of a chocolate cake which was smeared all over her face.

At this moment Nanny came in.

Seizing the little Princess, but careful to keep her at arm's length, her father said, "Take this child to her nursery at once!"

"With two such charming children, whom every one admires and wants to spoil, isn't it sometimes difficult?" I asked. The Duchess smiled and said, "No . . . you see, they have so many cousins to keep them in their places."

Our trip concluded with a week in Paris, the world's gayest city, where we spent New Year's Eve, and where, through the kindness of the Hon. Philippe Roy, Canadian Ambassador to France, and his Western Canadian wife, we met many interesting people and had the distinction of occupying the box of the President of the Republic of France at the opera.   ❧

Chapter XIX
MY "CAREER" BEGINS AT SEVENTY!

In January 1935, the year of the final session of Canada's seventeenth Parliament, because of serious illness George resigned as Speaker of the House of Commons. The Conservative Government, which had been swept into office in 1930, had administered the affairs of the country through one of the most difficult periods in Canadian as well as world history—the great depression. The Rt. Hon. R.B. Bennett would have to face a hostile electorate who apparently had expected his Government to perform economic miracles. The rumblings of the discontented voters were heard well in advance. It was a critical time. However, as usual, George and I went North—my first concern being to help hasten the restoration of his health.

Parliament prorogued. The Dominion election was announced. Quite evidently George was not well enough to face the rigours of a Yukon election campaign. It was decided that I should run in his place—as an Independent-Conservative. The frequently stated, half-jocular claim that in Yukon there are but two political parties—the Liberals and the Blacks—was now to be put to a test. I was to be the political pinch-hitter for George Black!

My campaign was different from any other in Canada. There were only 1,805 registered voters in a territory of over 200,000 square miles—the largest constituency in Canada in area and the smallest in population. There were no radio broadcasting stations. I held only seven public meetings. To reach voters I had to travel by plane, row and motor boat, steamer, two-horse team, and the old reliable "shank's mare." I once walked several miles to visit three voters, one of whom had declared himself "agin" me. But it was worth it, for those voters had to walk eight miles to vote. (I am told I got all three votes.) Another time my car got mired in two feet of mud, and I had to tramp miles to get assistance. In my river travels sometimes the engine of my small boat would go dead in mid-stream. This meant forced landings on uninhabited shores, where frequently we came upon herds of caribou, flocks of ptarmigan, or the odd bear cub, to which I could at least rehearse my campaign speeches without being heckled.

I had other troubles too. There were the younger women, who said, "What can this damned old woman do for us at Ottawa?" That was hard to take, yet I hurled back, "You'll be lucky when you reach my age if you have my sturdy legs, my good stomach, my strong heart, and what I like to call my headpiece."

The Conservative party was defeated overwhelmingly. However, I was successful in winning—by a 134 majority, which was considered "pretty good for a woman," especially a Conservative woman, in face of the Liberal landslide. I owe my success to the love and loyalty of our old friends, to personal canvassing, and to a split in the Liberal party!

On hearing of my election a feminine supporter of my opponent remarked bitterly, "She ran nothing but a sob-sister campaign." Well, what if I did. And I would have sobbed louder if necessary.

In Winnipeg, en route to Ottawa, I visited Lyman and his wife. A group of friends had gathered in their home on election night to hear the results over the radio.

"We listened until it was announced there would be no more returns that night," said Lyman's wife, "and we had no news from Yukon."

"Well, I guess poor old mother is another also ran," remarked Lyman.

In the morning Lyman called up the *Winnipeg Free Press,* asking, "Who got in in Yukon?" A voice passed the question on to someone else, who replied: "Oh, that other dame!"

Canada's eighteenth Parliament opened February 6, 1936. It was not only a momentous day in my life, but one of unusual historic significance. It was the first Canadian Parliament in the reign of the new monarch, King Edward VIII. There was a new Governor-General, Lord Tweedsmuir, who had been appointed as plain John Buchan, of world-wide literary fame. The Liberal party had been returned to power with the largest majority in the history of the country. But all hearts were deeply saddened by the Empire's loss of its beloved sovereign, King George V.

Guns, which twice within the previous fortnight had been hauled to the top of Parliament Hill, first to thunder a salute to the new King, later to fire 70 minute-guns (one gun per minute) the day of the late King's funeral, signalled the arrival of His Excellency Lord Tweedsmuir to open Parliament in the name of His Majesty King Edward VIII.

The Commons are assembled in their chamber to elect a Speaker. Sitting there, I am haunted by memories of other openings—before the war, during the regime of the Duke and Duchess of Connaught . . . during the war, after the fire of 1917, when Parliament met in the old museum, and the Duke and Duchess of Devonshire represented Their Majesties . . .Byng of Vimy and his clever, thoughtful wife . . . the Willingdons of India, those aristocrats of blood and commerce . . . the Bessboroughs, charming and delightful, the Countess so remarkably beautiful . . . and now, the first Baron and Baroness Tweedsmuir, both literary, he a former member of the British House of Commons.

How thrilled I had been in 1921 to see George actually take his seat in the Parliament of Canada. Other openings—1925, 1926—came to my mind, each making him more politically important. As a silent partner, as an onlooker, I was never happier than at the time of the 1930 opening, when he was elected Speaker. I enjoyed all attendant honours, as wife of the First Commoner.

I look at the Speaker's empty chair and my eyes fill with tears. If only he were in my seat! How the picture has changed for me! Now, at the age of 70, I am here alone.

I try to comfort myself by recalling life's many compensations. I call forth my old fighting spirit. I berate myself as a coward, unworthy to be trusted with the responsibility of my Yukon's representation. I think of the battle cry of the North, "Mush on!" "Mush on!" Service's lines come to me:

> *This is the law of the Yukon,*
> *And ever she makes it plain,*
> *Send not your feeble nor foolish,*
> *Send me your strong and your sane—*
> *Strong for the red rage of battle,*
> *Sane, for I harry them sore,*
> *Men who are girt for the combat,*
> *Men who are grit to the core.* *

---

*From *The Collected Poems of Robert Service,* by Robert Service; reprinted with permission of publishers Dodd, Mead & Company, Inc.

Now they are electing the Speaker—the Hon. P.F. Casgrain of Quebec, a well-known Frenchman. I know his wife, and the fight she is making for women's suffrage, still denied the women of that old French province.

The Gentleman Usher of the Black Rod, Major Drew Thompson, has come to summon us to hear the speech from the throne. Led by him, the Sergeant-at-Arms—the intrepid Major Gregg, V.C.—the Speaker, his page, the Clerk of the Commons— Dr. Arthur Beauchesne—the assistant clerk—the well-beloved Tom Fraser—and the members troop noisily to the bar of the Senate Chamber. His Excellency Lord Tweedsmuir reads the speech from the throne in English and French, Her Excellency, seated beside him, following it with radiant intelligence.

Although some of the customary colour and glitter of the opening is dimmed by court mourning—the black gowns and gloves of the women, the weepers of the judges of the Supreme Court, the black armbands on the blue and red uniforms of the military, naval, and air force officers—we look upon a brilliant scene.

The next day the Commons assembled to pass resolutions of sympathy to His Majesty King Edward VIII and the Queen Mother. Both the Rt. Hon. W.L. Mackenzie King, Prime Minister, and the Rt. Hon. R.B. Bennett, leader of the Opposition, spoke eloquently and sincerely. The Hon. Ernest Lapointe, French gentleman of Quebec, emotional to his fingertips, expressed poignantly, in his beautiful mother tongue, the grief of his confreres. J.H. Blackmore, leader of the new Social Credit party, and J.S. Woodsworth, of the Canadian Commonwealth Federation, voiced the sorrow of their groups.

As I listen I mourn, not so much for the new King who has lost his father, as for the Queen Mother who has lost her husband . . . her loneliness at this dark hour. I feel that the heart of every woman in Canada has gone out to her in deepest sympathy; that the women of Canada would wish her to know this; that perhaps I should express it for them. I hesitate, then write a note to Col. A.C. Casselman, Conservative party whip, asking, "Should I not say a word of sympathy on behalf of the women of Canada?"

"I think not," was his reply.

As the moments passed the urge to speak became greater. I could resist it no longer. My heart was too full. I arose. The silence of the room closed about me. I was afraid my voice would fail me. I prayed for courage to face that appalling hush. From my heart I said:

> "Mr. Speaker, it seems to me I should be derelict in my duty to the women of my beloved constituency in the North, and to the women of Canada generally, if I did not join my voice to the voices of the Rt. Hon. the Prime Minister and my Rt. Hon. Leader of the Opposition. Her Majesty the Queen has set the women of Canada an example of devotion to family, devotion to business that comes up every day—an example by which we must all profit. On behalf of the women of Canada I should like to be allowed to join in this tribute of regret and sympathy to that beautiful woman."

It was my first speech—my maiden speech—in the Parliament of Canada.

Two weeks later I celebrated my seventieth birthday. ✷

EPILOGUE

Twenty more fascinating years were to pass before Martha Louise died, at the age of 91, in Whitehorse on October 31, 1957.

As word of her death spread across the continent, messages came from royalty, prime ministers, parliamentary colleagues and old northern friends. Funeral services were held at the little Anglican Log Church in Whitehorse, with Bishop Tom Greenwood and the Reverend Arthur Privett officiating, and members of the Royal Canadian Mounted Police acting as a guard of honour.

Spunky to the end, Martha had decreed that both her flags should cover the coffin—the Stars and Stripes and the Union Jack. Her eye for the perfect detail had never failed, and the American Legion post at Skagway obliged by shipping the American flag to Whitehorse on the White Pass & Yukon Route, over the trail of '98 which Martha had conquered so many years before.

"A blithe spirit has left the Yukon," said the *Whitehorse Star* in its front page tribute reporting her funeral. "Martha Louise Black was the unrivalled queen of all that host of men and women who sought the northern magic . . . she, above all, caught and reflected the true spirit of the Yukon and some of it died with her."

A national news story outside began: "All Canada looked to the Yukon with a bow when Martha Black died."

At the opening session of Yukon Council a few days later, Commissioner Fred Collins paid tribute to his friend, saying, "Distinguished in the fields of art, letters, science and politics, and a figure of national importance . . . her life and career stand as an inspiration to all citizens of our nation in achievement under circumstances which might well have destroyed those charming attributes of her endearing personality."

What are some of those circumstances? Turn back again to her days in the House of Commons after her seventieth birthday.

* * * *

In October 1935, Martha had emerged victorious as the Independent-Conservative candidate in Yukon despite a Liberal landslide in the federal election. She had defeated Vancouver barrister J.P. Smith, a former Yukon resident, who ran as an Independent-Liberal, 681 to 556 votes out of a possible total of 1,805.

She assumed her seat in the House of Commons in February 1936, two weeks before her seventieth birthday, the second woman to be elected to the Canadian Parliament; Agnes McPhail of Ontario was the first. It was a familiar setting for Martha after 15 years in Ottawa with her husband. She had merely moved from the Gallery to the floor of the House, where she sat on the Opposition side. As the Speaker's wife, she had been involved in all the behind-the-scenes business of Parliament, privy to many secrets, and certainly was well qualified to join the club.

Faithful in attendance, she was in her appointed place daily, listened to all the debates, spoke when matters came up concerning Yukon, kept in touch with her constitutents by regular newsletters. But she obviously considered that she was just a substitute for the real thing, "keeping the seat warm for George." In her time, against her background and social training, that was to be expected, but it could be regretted from today's point of view. What could she not have accomplished, given a free rein as one of today's "liberated women"?

In her diary for January 1937, Martha wrote: "I am glad to be back but could very easily take a back seat and enjoy having George as M.P., not that I do not appreciate the place and the honour, yet I know that he would make a more desirable Member."

She was constantly worrying about George, ill and alone in Vancouver. She confided: "I dread leaving George; he is blue and at more or less loose ends; I only hope he will be able to work up enough of an office practice so that we may have a home and live a comfortably settled life. I would be happy to have a few friends and live away from the crowds—reading, writing, and doing some flower work. I wonder!"

She was busy with her co-author, Elizabeth Bailey Price, selecting photos to illustrate her forthcoming book, *My Seventy Years*, and its serialization in *Chatelaine* magazine, which had paid her an advance of $250 for 50,000 words. Things were going well for Martha.

But February 1937 ushered in a time of disaster. McClelland & Stewart, her Toronto publishers, decided to turn down the book; so died the serial due to begin in the March issue of *Chatelaine*. Eventually, Thomas Nelson published *My Seventy Years*.

Martha kept plugging away as Member of Parliament. She spoke at 11 o'clock one night in the House, suggesting the minting of special silver medals for the coronation, and noted in her diary the next day: "Read over my speech in Hansard this morning . . . seems fairly decent, but the Minister of Finance, Dunning, explained very nicely why coronation coins could not be issued in time." On her birthday that month, she received a corsage of orchids from her fellow Conservative M.P.'s, and a cordial letter from R.B. Bennett, former Prime Minister, now sitting in Opposition. Then came one of her blackest days.

On February 27, her youngest son, Capt. Lyman Black, was killed in a car crash while driving from Kingston to Ottawa with an Army friend. It was a cruel trick of fate that he should meet death in the quiet Ontario countryside after surviving the hazards of World War I. His young wife, Aimee, was staying with Martha in Ottawa and the two women had been looking forward to welcoming him for the weekend.

Martha Louise tried piteously to be brave in order to comfort her daughter-in-law. She carried on through the next dark days, but the light had gone out of her life. In her diary she wrote: "I am lonely. I feel bowed and broken for the first time in my life. . . . I can never forget the comfort Lyman was to me two years ago when George was taken sick. He was a very tower of strength."

But hard work had always been her solace, and on March 12 she wrote: "Spoke for 25 minutes in the House, on Yukon. A splendid reception and hearing in the Chamber; all Members most receptive." March 15: "At the House. Carried on as usual. Some days I feel fresh and able to go on—on others it is with great difficulty that I can whip myself up to take any interest in people or my work, but that will never do." March 17: "I seem to have lost my grip. I am tired when I get up, tired when I go to bed—tired in mind and body." And through it all ran her love and praise of Aimee, whom she described as heart-broken but brave.

Perhaps this helps explain why, in an interview for the *Buffalo Evening News* that same month, Martha was quoted as saying: "I wonder if women, for the very reason that they are women, can quite shoulder their full responsibilities in a public manner? Woman's chief mission is not administering artificial respiration to a dying world, nor working perspiringly in a forward movement. Into the life of every woman that is well ordered, come those years of child-bearing and child-rearing. For this reason, most women must defer activity in politics until middle life."

The interview went on to say that the fact that "marriage is to a man a thing in part and woman's whole existence" explained to Mrs. Black why more Canadian women were not wearing their new political hats; and recalling the fatigues of campaigning, the bitterness and the disappointment which must always be the lot of some candidate in any battle of the ballots, she wondered how any woman really wanted to face the drudgery of long hours of concentration on statistics "dry as dust."

Martha was still recovering from Lyman's death, back in Dawson for the summer, when news came of the death of her first-born, Warren Grafton Purdy, on August 17, 1937, at the age of 48.

The following January, she and Aimee took up residence at 251 Cooper Street in Ottawa for the parliamentary session, "as paying guests . . . $125 per month for two rooms, bath, breakfast, dinners Saturdays and Wednesdays, all meals on Sundays." On February first came the news that her only brother, George Merrick Munger, Jr., had died in the State Tuberculosis Hospital at Salem, Oregon. It was George with whom she had climbed the Chilkoot Trail, who had bought her a warm meal and a fire at the summit, cheered her on through the rough spots, comforted her when her baby was born in Dawson, shared the Klondike days with her. Another tough blow for Martha.

But the following day, she spoke for 30 minutes in the House about her beloved Yukon, and confided in her diary, "As nervous as a witch—very tired when I finished." A week later she was speaking at Women's Canadian Club luncheons in western Ontario cities, London, Statford, St. Catharines. Always in demand as a speaker, she probably graced more luncheon and banquet head tables than any other woman of her time, and her charming, poised exterior gave never a hint of the worry and sadness hidden from the world.

Every compliment, every bright spot, was treasured, however. At the beginning of her 1938 diary she wrote: "Clem Burns sent me a letter he had received from Robert Service [the poet of the Yukon] in which he said, 'I am sorry that George Black is not so well. He was one of the finest of sports. I cannot believe Mrs. B. is 70. In the old days she was like a marquise with a note of finish and distinction.' Well, even tho I am 70, I am still vain enough to lap up them few kind words!"

The regular report she made to Yukoners in March of 1939 shows her clear grasp of what went on in the House: "The Speech from the Throne was longer than usual this year and contained the same amount of general information—which means practically nothing. About two weeks were wasted by the House in discussing the Speech, following which we were plunged almost immediately into a discussion of the Bren Gun contract scandal and the Davis Commission which investigated. . . .

"An amusing little incident occurred in the House a week or ten days ago when Mr. Power, Minister of Pensions and National Health, brought down a resolution to control drugs, cosmetics, etc. One of the Social Credit members got up and asked silly questions about the use of cosmetics, finally asking the Minister to give him the weight of lipstick. It was so ridiculous that I stood on my feet and demonstrated the use of powder from my compact and suggested that all we wanted was to have protection against poisonous powders and cosmetics. Someone said afterwards that it was a relief to have the discussion changed from gunpowder to face powder. . . .

"The Main Estimates have been brought down. They are not entirely satisfactory to Yukon, but I am assured that Yukon will be taken care of in the Supplementary Estimates, which I hope is so. . . .

"I receive so many invitations to speak before churches and clubs. In a few days I am going to Belleville with the Liberal Member to speak before an evening meeting of the Rotary Club and show our films of the Yukon. I am using them again in other constituencies at the request of Members of both political parties. [These old glass slides are in the Yukon Archives at Whitehorse.]

"I will write again before the Session closes and hope to be able to report that more appreciable progress has been made by the Government toward solving the important problems confronting the people of Canada and the Canadian taxpayer than has been made to date. . . ."

Martha was really an independent, politically; it mattered not whether she spoke with a Liberal on the same platform beside her. Some 10 years later, with George back in harness as Yukon M.P., she attended a dinner in the parliamentary restaurant to honour two members of the Progressive Conservative party who had served 25 years in the House. Reporting the event, the *Toronto Evening Telegram* said: "Little Mrs. Martha Louise Black stole the show at the John Bracken dinner. . . . Behind the frail little grey-haired woman are the vast spreads of the Yukon . . . and when she smilingly said to John Bracken, 'I represent no party; I represent the people of the Yukon,' she received the main ovation of the evening from a hard-boiled audience."

Nor was she a nationalist. In Emily Kendall Wheeldon's interview for the *Buffalo Evening News* in 1937, her views were sought because she represented American-Canadian backgrounds, but the reporter wrote: "I soon realized that her interest transcends both her American birth and her Canadian citizenship. She hates that sectionalism and all its works which divide man from his brother man.

"All nationalism is an obsession born of fear, declared this descendant of men who fought under Washington. Women are not going to tolerate such an anomaly as war in a boastedly-civilized world. Anything, however, trifling, that creates a better understanding between peoples, ceases to be trifling."

On her way home to Yukon from Ottawa, in March 1940, interviewed by the *Alaska Weekly* in Juneau, Martha was most emphatic about the need for an international highway. "It will be built when both Canada and the United States want it badly enough." She was right. The Alaska Highway was built as a wartime joint effort two years later, but it didn't follow the route she had hoped for, which would have brought it through Dawson and Mayo from Alaska, then to Whitehorse.

During that Juneau interview, when asked to comment on the suggestion that British Columbia should join Yukon, Mrs. Black exploded. "God forbid!" she shouted. "Do you want us in the Yukon to pay British Columbia's bills?"

Just about the strongest pronouncement from Martha on the subject of women in Parliament came in an interview published in *Toronto Saturday Night,* in March 1924, when she was the wife of the Yukon M.P. "The House of Commons sat long this year.

I have never been an ardent suffragist, but the longer I live the more I realize that women couldn't do any worse than the 200-odd so-called statesmen that Canada sends to Ottawa each year."

Her outspoken frankness carried over into her writing, which she continued through the years for many Canadian publications. "The veriest drivel I ever read," she confided to her diary one day about a book on Alaska she had been invited to review. During their months in Vancouver between sessions, when George was off at the Pittmeadow Gun Club hunting game birds, she would work over some old Yukon stories. "Hope to be able to brush them up for either the *Province* or *Chatelaine.*" The Blacks always needed money and were too generous for their own good when they had it.

In addition to *My Seventy Years*, her book *Yukon Wild Flowers* (illustrated by George Black's photographs), and the numerous little booklets she wrote for benefit of the I.O.D.E., Martha authored the Joe Boyle story for *Delineator* magazine, among other published work, and was professional enough in her approach to become a member of the Canadian Authors Association. Sitting in the House, listening to interminable debates, Martha sometimes blocked out another story for *Canadian Home Journal*, or the *I.O.D.E. Echoes*. She was offered the national presidency of the Imperial Order in 1931, and confided to her diary, "It hardly seems possible such an honour could come to me—it must be carefully considered." But she turned it down.

Part of the year in Ottawa, part in Vancouver, part in Dawson—that was the pattern for many years, and Martha commented in 1931: "Packing-packing-packing. A most harrowing operation several times a year. I would like to feel I would someday have a real home—it is a trying life to go hither and yon all the time and yet I am genuinely thankful for all the mercies vouchsafed me."

With George recovered and back in Ottawa as Yukon Member once again, Whitehorse began to supercede Dawson City as the economic centre of the Territory because of its location at the hub of the transportation wheel, on the Alaska Highway, White Pass & Yukon railway, Yukon River, and main airways. George found his law practice dwindling in Dawson, and in August 1944 bought a home in Whitehorse, into which they moved that autumn. The First Avenue bungalow had been built in 1903 and first occupied

About to board a White Pass & Yukon train on their way to Ottawa, George and Martha Black have a few final words with old friend Judge Jack Gibben.

The George Black residence at the corner of First Avenue and Jarvis Street, Whitehorse, as it was when Martha spent her last years there.

148

by the grandparents of present-day northern pilot Bud Harbottle. Later owned by T.C. Richards of hotel fame, it has been considered one of the finest homes in town. Once settled in, the Blacks opened their house to everyone from far and near, as they had in Dawson, or London or Ottawa or Vancouver. The I.O.D.E. began holding their regular meetings there, with Martha in their midst except when she joined George in Ottawa for winter sessions of Parliament. Coming north each summer, they would visit Mayo and Dawson City, travelling on riverboats as long as they ran, flying in later years.

The end of their travelling days came in 1949 when George announced his retirement from politics, no longer standing as a Yukon candidate for federal election. He kept busy with his law practice, fishing and hunting with his many old cronies throughout the Territory. Martha settled happily into a social routine, tea hour visitors, meetings of her church, Red Cross, and I.O.D.E. groups, and they both kept up a lively interest in everything going on around them. Martha's correspondence continued to be voluminous enough to require a secretary who came three evenings a week and took dictation from her.

Old age was beginning to take its toll. One day, alone in the house, Martha was making herself some toast when the curtains above the toaster ignited, blazed up, and started what became a serious fire. She was burned trying to beat out the flames, and was several weeks convalescing at the Regina Hotel, in the same block as their home, while repairs and reconstruction went on. At that time, an office and waiting room were added for George, and a large new kitchen.

Several falls and a fractured hip later, she was forced to use a wheelchair, which frustrated her but didn't prevent her from getting out to meetings and parties. Old friends such as G.I. Cameron would lift her into a car, carry her into her destination, bring along the wheelchair, and take her home again. Martha was fortunate in obtaining the services of a housekeeper for many years, and close friends called daily and helped in many ways.

She had been listed in the Dominion Day honours in 1948 with the award of the Order of the British Empire "for cultural and social contributions to the Yukon," but there was no opportunity for the actual presentation until the following March when she was in Victoria, staying at the Priory Guest House after hospitalization.

Here is her account of that highlight in her life, from the letter she wrote George the night of the ceremonial dinner, March 26, 1949:

"My Husband: The day passed, the evening followed suit and now the night seems but as a dream. A telephone message during the morning was to the effect, Government House wishes to speak to Mrs. Black. On going to the telephone the voice of His Honour, Lieutenant-Governor Charles Banks said, 'How are you feeling this morning? Bunty wishes to speak with you for a moment,' followed by the rich, full voice of the chatelaine of Government House. Again a pleasantly solicitous enquiry as to my health—after all I had spent a recent month in hospital but it was too much to expect a busy Lieutenant-Governor and his equally engaged wife to remember.

"'Remember we are expecting you this evening' (as though I could possibly forget an invitation to Government House with a notation—'In Honour to His Excellency, the Governor-General'). My taxi drew up in front of the Priory Guest House promptly at 20 minutes after seven. As the dinner was announced for 7:45 I gave myself ample time allowing for a possible hit and run driver, but all was well and I arrived safely under the porte cochere in due course to be greeted by the attendant. I was the first guest, so had ample time to change my slippers, titivate a little and be ready to go to the drawing room when a messenger came to announce that His Honour and Mrs. Banks would like to see me.

"I was really excited and flustered, far more so than in earlier days when such occasions were more or less of daily occurrence.

"On entering the drawing room, His Honour and Mrs. Banks greeted me as though I really belonged, while they explained to me just the part I was to play in the pre-dinner ceremony.

"When the Governor-General entered the room, all the guests were arranged on an opposite side while His Honour and Mrs. Banks stood in front of me and presented me to His Excellency. A small table stood at the head of the drawing room on which was a cushion, a leather-covered box and two cardboard scrolls. His Honour gave me his hand and presented me to His Excellency, the Governor-General. The aide read my citation, and His Excellency pinned the O.B.E. on my left upper chest. I made my curtsey and in a few moments we were all served a delicious cocktail—and DID I need it—I'll tell the world I did. In the meantime, in an undertone I had said to His Honour 'If this lasts much longer I will burst into tears' . . . possibly for a moment he believed me, for shaking his head he whispered, 'You must NOT.' I managed a fairly decent curtsey (difficult with my game legs) and all was over.

"Dinner was announced . . . at the table my eyes were rivetted on, first, the men who served us—all returned men and all with from one to three rows of ribbons. I could not but compare my foolish pride over my new decoration won by simply living, with those ribbons worn with simplicity by men who had fought and endured that we might live. . . .

"You have wondered probably why you have not seen an account of the investiture and the state dinner in the papers. Several reporters came to me asking if I would tell them about the evening, but with my experience with 'The Great Ones of the World' I knew that any information, under such circumstances, should come from the fountainhead of knowledge — which in this instance would be His Honour the Lieutenant-Governor and Mrs. Banks. I am writing to you all these small details because of the interest you naturally have had, and I know that you will treat this letter as confidential; if any information should be given, it must not come from either you or me.

"The decoration is really very beautiful. As you know, I was given permission to wear the miniature as soon as the award had been announced. I would feel particularly pleased if, when you had the opportunity, you would tell the Hon. Paul Martin that I shall never forget the part he played in having the award made to me.

"I shall be looking forward to your arrival here after

Easter Sunday and hope that you will remain for some time. You may possibly have seen the spring copy of *Echoes*. If so, you will I hope read 'Yukon Journey,' by Barbara E. Osler. Twice in the article she speaks very generously of me.

"This has been a long letter, my dear Husband, and in a manner, difficult to write, for there was so much that was comfortably delightful to look back at. I am sending a copy of this to Donald, to His Honour the Lieutenant-Governor and Mrs. Banks. Beyond that, to no other friend or relative unless given permission to do so. Looking forward to seeing you shortly. Your wife, M.L.B."

And in her own handwriting, Martha added a line to say:

"Government House released the story later."

Later that same year, at Christmas 1949, George was listed among the New Year's honours as a member of the Privy Council, an award which his political friends had been urging for some years. Greetings and congratulations came from many old friends.

Having adopted George Black's church as well as his nationality and politics, Martha became a member of the Anglican Church of Canada (Episcopal in the States). A member and officer of the Woman's Auxiliary for many years, she was the proud wearer of the gold Winchester Cross, symbol of her life membership in that organization. In her eighties, she happily attended such functions as diocesan jubilee celebrations of the W.A. at Whitehorse. (After her death, her pin was presented to me with a life membership from the Diocese of Yukon, and is a treasured possession.)

In the spring of 1954, on repeated urgings from Martha, the pasque flower, or crocus, was adopted as the Territorial floral emblem. She had always loved the furry little flower which was the first to poke through the snows of winter to reassure a waiting world that spring would come soon; she preferred it to the flashier magenta fireweed universally known throughout the North. Territorial Council was well aware of the fact that the crocus had been Manitoba's floral emblem for some years, but because of their admiration and respect for Mrs. Black, the local expert on wild flowers of the Yukon, they quietly waited until after her death to revoke their choice and name the fireweed (*Epilobium angustifolium*), the Yukon flower instead.

The same kind of indirect approach was adopted when the time came to tell the Hon. George Black, K.C., P.C., that he couldn't renew his driver's license. How do you tell a stubborn octogenarian, accustomed to being in charge of the situation, that he is no longer competent behind the wheel—especially when he was one of the first drivers of an automobile in the Yukon? The R.C.M.P. had so many complaints about George backing out into other vehicles, which he neither saw nor heard, they had to remove him from the streets as a public menace, but they passed the assignment to Commissioner Collins. He wrote the official letter, which was a masterpiece of diplomacy and sweet reason, but even so, Fred Collins delivered the letter by hand and had a drink over it with George.

Five years after retirement from politics, the Blacks were still considered "Mr. and Mrs. Yukon" by most Northerners. On George's eighty-first birthday, the *Whitehorse Star* reviewed his career, extended congratulations, and described him as "Yukon's outstanding citizen, and in his service and contribution to this northland shares first place honours only with his wife, the gracious First Lady of the Yukon, Martha Louise."

On her eighty-eighth birthday in 1954, Martha received 60 guests, the usual bouquets and telegrams of greeting from all parts of Canada. She and George were guest speakers at the I.O.D.E. annual banquet a week later when a very special birthday cake was presented. Captain Black took the salute at the Remembrance Day parade that November 11; he and Martha were Patron and Patroness of the Yukon Historical Society; together they attended the Yukon premiere of the new film "The Far Country" as guests of the owner of the Yukon Theatre in Whitehorse.

The following year the pattern was much the same: another birthday party, social events, callers; visitors who came to see the Yukon wanted to include the First Lady as one of the special points of interest on their tour, and Martha received them all. In that summer of 1955 one of the highlights was attending the ninety-first birthday of their old friend Isaac Taylor, one of the founders of Taylor & Drury department stores in Yukon, who had walked in over the trail of '98 but stopped before reaching Dawson. It was a happy family gathering at the summer home of his son, C. D. Taylor, on the beach at Marsh Lake.

That August 1,500 Sourdoughs were expected to converge on Eureka, California, for their annual reunion, and though unable to attend, Martha Louise contributed her own sourdough recipe for the occasion, used since her first days in Dawson. Martha's hot cakes really did melt in the mouth, and her early fame as a cook in Dawson City was based on them and her home-baked beans.

That September, George and Martha enjoyed their last stern-wheeler ride, on board the SS *Tutshi*, sailing with a Masonic Lodge charter from Carcross to the beautiful garden spot of Ben-My-Chree. The Blacks had known the original residents, Mr. and Mrs. Otto Partridge, and it was a nostalgic experience to see the place without them. However, some of Martha's pressed-flower pictures were on display there, as a gift from the Canadian Pacific Railway, which brightened her up considerably. It was the last season the *Tutshi* was afloat; the paddlewheeler has been up on dry land at Carcross ever since and is now protected as a historic site.

Although both in their eighties, the Blacks kept in the social swim. They had become close friends of Commissioner and Mrs. Collins, visiting back and forth, reminiscing over the old guest register from the Dawson Commissioner's house, which Sybil Collins put back into official use. Many tales were inspired by the signatures in the old book, most of them not for publication!

In January 1965, a month after Martha's ninetieth birthday, Austin Cross of the *Ottawa Citizen*, writing of his visit to the Yukon, reported that he arrived on the train at Whitehorse at midnight and was met by Fred and Sybil Collins, "and we promptly took off at 12:05 to call on Hon. George Black, former Speaker of the Commons, and the gracious and unforgettable Martha Black." Later in January, the Blacks flew to Vancouver for a holiday at The Devonshire, and George was guest speaker at the Sourdough meeting there, which brought forth this comment in the group's newsletter: "The contribution that Mr. and Mrs. Black have made to the Yukon and the Canadian way of life has won for them a place in Canadian history for all time and a very special place in the hearts of all sourdoughs!"

Home again in Whitehorse, the two old diehards co-signed a letter to the *Star* on February second, referring to an article in the *Atlantic Monthly* regarding wildlife areas being taken over by

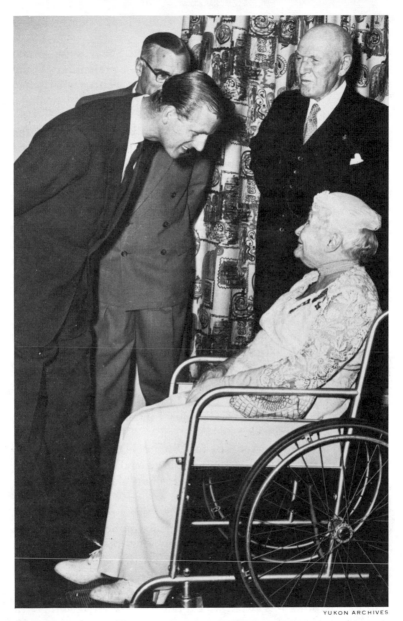

Mr. and Mrs. George Black with the then Duke of Edinburgh at Whitehorse in 1954. In the background stands Yukon Commissioner Wilf Brown.

military groups. They applied it to a similar happening in Yukon and signed off: "Yours for public liberty!"

February 1956 was a big month for Martha. She was the special guest at the I.O.D.E. Founders Day banquet, a preliminary to the grand celebration of the ninetieth birthday on February 24, when 100 guests called during the afternoon and evening to pay homage, admire the floral offerings, read the telegrams of greeting, and sip the traditional Tom and Jerry punch mixed expertly for the occasion by old-timers Emil Forrest and G. I. Cameron. Displayed in a prominent place was a photograph with her latest conquest—H.R.H. the Duke of Edinburgh, bending down to chat with her during his recent Yukon visit. The two had hit it off admirably, Martha with a gleam in her eye for this handsome young man, and H.R.H. enjoying her repartee.

Naturally her ninetieth birthday made the news across Canada and she was interviewed by press and radio people. Her birthday message in the *Whitehorse Star* said: "As time goes on, it seems to me that only the happy days remain. There were troubles, there were hardships that at moments seemed unbearable, but they have all been forgotten, only the pleasant remain."

In a longer interview, which I taped for the Trans-Canada network of the Canadian Broadcasting Corporation, Martha told how she spent her days, stuck in a wheelchair, planning a new edition of her book to be called *My Ninety Years*, and added: "I do nothing but sit and think. . . . if I had the ability of former years, I might do more than think. I realize now I should have done a great deal more."

She had flown to Dawson City for Discovery Day celebrations the previous August 17 and was upset at the general state of decay and neglect. "Dawson is a wreck. I saw three of my old homes . . . it just made me heartsick."

As she travelled back through her memories, Mrs. Black confided details which she had not included in her book, perhaps from a sense of ladylike delicacy so many years before, or perhaps embroidering the story after so many misty years. "That first winter in Dawson, when I discovered I was to have another baby, it struck me with horror. I was attended by two men, a one-armed man and the other was an old sea captain. They were so gentle with me. The one-armed man had a big hook for a hand, wrapped around with cotton . . . very soft . . . and so the baby was born."

JAMES WHYARD

Three First Ladies of the Yukon: Martha Louise Black, Sibyl Collins, and Lena Gibson, each the wife of a Commissioner of the Yukon. The photograph was taken in the former Commissioner's residence in Valleyview before the present building in Riverdale was constructed.

JAMES WHYARD

Old friends were on hand to reminisce with Martha on her ninetieth birthday. Here, Trail of '98 veteran Isaac Taylor, founder of Taylor & Drury pioneer merchants, and his son Charles visit with Mrs. Black.

157

Martha continued: "I was in need of a lawyer's services and a post office official, Doug Edwards, recommended George Black to me as a lawyer. 'He hasn't a big practice and won't overcharge,' he said. During one of our conversations, Mr. Black commented on conduct of mine to which he objected. I told him, 'I'm paying you for legal advice . . . if I need any other kind I will ask for it!' He told me later he could have spanked me!

"I was raised to believe that a woman's place was in the home, and only ran for M.P. because my husband was ill. Later my husband was re-elected, much to my delight."

Her final message to Canadian women, their husbands, and children, on that day was: "Meet each day as it comes, and remember, you must do what you know to be right. I haven't always done so, but have been given grace to make amends." And she said, wistfully, "Young women of the present day have so many opportunities to make something of themselves."

Long forgotten was an earlier message of inspiration, published in the year-end edition of the *Vancouver Province* during the "hungry thirties" and the great depression. Martha wrote: "The women of Canada in this New World today are facing problems that were unknown to their pioneer grandmothers. True, those women of one hundred and more years ago had no electric light, running water (save in streams that passed their door) motor cars or other luxuries that we of the present call necessities, yet the very difficulties of their lives gave them a sturdiness of mind and body that we of today seem to lack. The present crisis arising from war, revolution, failure of crops, mass production, transportation problems, over-population coupled with ignorance in many countries, a mad orgy of crime in congested centres, an indifference to public duty by both men and women, the demand of those of small means for the luxuries of the wealthy, all tend to make the present situation more difficult to deal with than the so-called depressions of the past.

"If, as statisticians tell us, the women of this country have the control and spending of from 60 to 85% of the money of this country, then it is distinctly our business to bear our share of the burden of the present trouble, which we can do by devotion to duty, determination to grapple with each problem understandingly, in the God-given knowledge that 'This too shall pass away.' "

As for political savvy, in her 1931 diary while fence-mending on

Martha and former Commissioner Fred Collins at her ninetieth birthday party.

George and Martha Black celebrate Martha's ninety-first birthday at her home in Whitehorse with close friends Fred and Sibyl Collins.

159

the Mayo hustings with George, Martha wrote: "Plenty of complaints about the political situation. It is a case of damned if you do and damned if you don't . . . the only thing to do is listen to all, then decide what you think is right. Then do it, regardless!"

Throughout the years, Martha's regard for George as a politician never wavered. At prorogation of the House in August 1931, she wrote: "George certainly looked his part as Speaker and has done well through a difficult session." How difficult, only she knew.

Perhaps it was a happier time for wives of politicians than in present days, but Martha always enjoyed the campaigning and the political power. When George spoke on a Vancouver radio station in 1931, she noted in her diary: "I listened in at the Savages . . . very much pleased. George has a splendid radio voice, smooth, perfect enunciation." She kept her own counsel when things went wrong, confiding very few of her serious problems even to her diary. Occasionally there would be an outraged moment, when a revealing sentence made it all too clear that she was not deceived by anything around her, but she gave the outside world no sign.

When Frances Parkinson Keyes came to write her life story in Ottawa, Martha told her diary: "The strange, sad history of me life . . . it is a weird one and would be more so if the half could be told." Of the American novelist herself, Martha said: "A clever , brilliant, interesting woman—but she must live a hectic life." Later, Martha was invited to lecture in the States through Mrs. Keyes' efforts.

After Martha's ninetieth birthday, George gave up his law practice that spring, turning it over to a newcomer in Whitehorse, Henry Regehr. That April saw another highlight—Canada's Governor-General, Vincent Massey, called at the Blacks' for tea and a private visit during his official tour of the north.

Sybil Collins, who with her husband was very much involved in the official arrangements for His Excellency's visit, recalls that day.

"On this famous occasion she asked me to select her dress, so I had an opportunity to see her wardrobe . . . many of them originals and all of them pretty. Some were by now too small, but there were plenty to choose from. I thought she looked beautiful on all occasions, but maybe handsome on this day, as she was really excited about Massey's visit.

"The Governor-General started the conversation with compliments, which she gracefully returned. Finally, he said, 'And I understand you and George have lived here, and been married for

At Martha's ninety-first birthday gathering, old friends Martha and G.I. Cameron flank Fred Collins in the back row, and George Black and Mrs. Collins are seated on each side of Martha. Seated in the background at right is Yukon Member of Parliament Erik Nielsen, later Deputy Prime Minister of Canada.

Martha Louise and Governor-General Vincent Massey chat over tea during his official tour of Yukon Territory in 1956. With them are Commissioner and Mrs. Fred Collins and George Black, in their Whitehorse home.

161

over 60 years?' She answered: 'Yes, Your Excellency, that is true, and if I may be permitted to say, it's been a hell of a long time!' She said such things to shock, but it never shocked the Yukoners. On this occasion, she did shock the Governor-General, who obviously was not prepared for that coming from such a dainty old lady!"

Mrs. Collins recalls other highlights of their friendship.

"Until we were well known and safely launched in the Yukon, our happiest times were with the Blacks. They made up with us instantly and we had no problems with either of them. On one occasion Martha said I was more like her in outlook than any of the Yukon ladies who followed after her. I was surprised to hear this, and she added, 'It's your great curiosity and interest in people' . . . she said she always had those qualities.

"On our early visits, we would place our coats on her bed, and I would see pictures from floor to ceiling, mostly photographs and all signed. Once, thinking I was alone, I rushed over to see them, and hearing a rustle, looked up to see Martha there in her wheelchair, laughing. She said, 'Having a gander?' I was all confusion, but admitted it. Then she said, 'Well, never be ashamed of it—half the world are too dead to see what's there in front of them.'

"When the Blacks visited us, they amused themselves. I would put out a tray with glasses and what goes in them. They would then ask for the old Government House guest books, and as they recalled the names from early days they would exchange laughing memories, obviously happy as larks with what they remembered. On one occasion, George started to write beside some of the names in the book and I assumed he was explaining who they were. Later, when they had gone, I discovered he had written in 'bastard' after all his old political enemies . . . in pencil, and I had to erase maybe a dozen such labels! We really should have taped those visits, when they would be recalling far-off history. . . . They would fall silent when they came to Lyman's signature. He would be 8 or 9 years old then, judging by the childish scrawl. . . . "

There were other lost opportunities. The CBC considered flying Martha out to Winnipeg for a television interview, which would have been a wonderful thing to see now, but plans fell through.

Martha's last year was fairly quiet. Her ninety-first birthday was observed in the traditional way, and she commented, "Still a good party!" but in later months, she went out of the house rarely. She died October 31, 1957.

The Royal Canadian Mounted Police acted as honor guards at Martha's funeral. Her coffin bore two flags: the Union Jack and the Stars and Stripes.

Martha's headstone in the Masonic section of the old Whitehorse cemetery on Sixth Avenue should have read born Mercer, Pennsylvania, 1866.

Shortly after Martha's funeral, George was joined in Whitehorse by his longtime friend, Sadie King, widow of a Vancouver building contractor. She helped him dispose of his local property and household effects, and took him back to Vancouver where they were married. The second Mrs. Black took good care of the venerable Yukoner in his failing years.

The Hon. George Black died in Shaughnessy Hospital there on August 23, 1965, at the age of 92. The *Vancouver Province* headed the story: "Brave Heart of the Yukon Finally Lets Go." Funeral services were held from Christ Church Cathedral with burial at Forest Lawn. In its last tribute, the *Province* did him proud:

"All the world loves a fighter. And when Capt. George Black moved into the federal political arena in Canada's tough northland in 1921 he proved himself. He was carrying the banner of the Conservative party at a time when Tory hopes were slim. And it was a desperate fight under desperate northern conditions. Once, while trying to reach Dawson, partly by car and partly by canoe, Black paddled a 100-mile stretch of open river until he was stopped by ice running bank-high. He abandoned river travel, hired a guide and snowshoed 150 miles through unbroken wilderness to a miner's camp. There he got a dog team and finally reached Dawson in 40-below weather.

"It was this type of campaigning that caught the admiration of the Yukoners, people still filled with the adventurous traditions of the land, and Black changed what looked like certain defeat into a spectacular victory.

"Born in Woodstock, New Brunswick, Black graduated in law and hung out his shingle to practice. He was an ambitious young man with a gift of speech, and politics were already in his blood. He had been called upon to campaign for the Conservative cause and had proved himself. Then, in 1898, word came of the Klondike gold strike. Only 25, he closed his office, collected what money he could lay his hands on and joined the stampede. He went after gold and did pretty well. He made a sudden fortune in a frozen creek and lost it as swiftly when the spring thaw sent floods through the diggings. Then he cut wood for riverboats, became a helmsman on a paddlewheeler and finally quit to go back to law in Dawson City. Within a few years he was political force in the new north country."

Let George himself add a few details to that brief outline. In answer to a request from writer Harold Hilliard for a *Toronto Star*

Weekly feature in 1955, George sent the following telegram: "In March, 1898 bought eight horses and sleds in Vancouver, hauled goods from Skagway to Log Cabin on White Pass right-of-way. Sold all but one horse; thence to Tagish Lake where camped, cut trees, whipsawed lumber, built scow and lapstreak boat, installed woodburning pipe boiler and propeller brought with party from Fredericton, New Brunswick.

"Spent summer of '98 prospecting on Big Salmon River. In August '99 made rich gold discovery there. Mined until fall of 1900. Went to Dawson City with gold. Presented barrister's credentials from New Brunswick bar, paid fee, admitted Yukon bar. Worked way to Dawson as deckhand on river steamboat. Owners had no money to pay officers and crew of boat so we sued in Admiralty Court. Sheriff sold boat and cargo under Seaman's Lien Law, paid all wages.

"Then more steamboats on Yukon River than traffic warranted and many owners unable to pay wages officers and crew. Having made reputation as first Admiralty lawyer in Yukon, officers and crews of other boats retained me to collect their wages on percentage which netted me over $3,500 and began successful law practice.

"When Dawson like all placer gold mining camps quieted down, population dwindled and Whitehorse created capital of Yukon, moved there, purchased residence, built addition for law office and continue to carry on."

After Martha's death, I.O.D.E. friend Mrs. W. D. MacBride worked hard to interest a publisher in bringing out a new edition of *My Seventy Years*, without success. She did, however, obtain from George Black a letter turning over all rights to the book, for the benefit of the Imperial Order Daughters of the Empire, because it had been one of Martha's favourite projects all through the years. On the occasion of their fiftieth and sixtieth wedding anniversaries, the Blacks had said no gifts, please, but contributions to the church or the I.O.D.E. would be accepted gratefully, and this rule also applied on all Martha's birthdays.

So now, with the publication of this new edition of her story, the royalties which she would have received will go to the I.O.D.E. for years to come, furthering some of the programs which she felt were valuable in maintaining the standards she held so high.

It is time for new generations of Northerners to read her story and absorb some of their heritage from the experiences lived in its pages. Gone now are the Klondykers who walked in over the trail of '98 with Martha Louise and George and all the other good companions. Gone are the annual Christmas gatherings, when she would collect a dozen lonely, old bachelors around her festive board. Gone is their home on the bank of the Yukon River, long empty, and victim of two final fires.

Gone is the Martha Louise Black Reading Room in the Yukon Territorial Library, its antiques and flower pictures removed when an addition was built to house the new Yukon Archives, in which, fortunately, some of her scrapbooks, letters, and photos are preserved. It is hoped that as word spreads, more and more of her belongings, which were spirited away and often treasured by old friends, will be returned to the MacBride Museum, or the Old Log Church Museum in Whitehorse, and that her other papers and manuscripts will be complete in the Archives.

At Dawson City, National Historic Sites plans the restoration of the handsome old Commissioner's residence, complete with the furnishings Martha chose. In the Dawson Museum, a display case holds treasured copies of several of her diaries, her prayer book, other small mementos. In Whitehorse, Black Street commemorates the well-known husband and wife team which played a star turn on the Canadian political stage.

There are two mountains in the Yukon named for Martha and George, as other peaks have received the names of Yukon pioneers.

What was Martha Louise really like? In her last years, her greeting to visitors would be, "Well, what's new?" And, frustrated by physical failings, she would say, "Isn't it hell to get old!" But pasted in one of her early diaries there is a clipping of a poem, from somewhere, which presents a truer picture of that wonderful person, as others saw her in those final years:

> *Let me grow lovely, growing old,*
> *So many fine things to do;*
> *Silks and ivory and gold*
> *And lace, need not be new.*
> *There is a magic in old trees,*
> *Old books a glamour hold.*
> *Why may not I, as well as these*
> *Grow lovely, growing old?*